1314

THE BATTLE OF
BANNOCKBURN

JOYCE MILLER

D1460666

GOBLINSHEAD

First Edition 2014
© Martin Coventry & Joyce Miller 2014
Battle plans © Duncan Jones

Published by
GOBLINSHEAD

130B Inveresk Road, Musselburgh EH21 7AY, Scotland
Tel: 0131 665 2894 Email: goblinshead@sol.co.uk

British Library Cataloguing in Publication Data
A catalogue record for this book is available from
the British Library.
ISBN 9781899874606
Typeset by **GOBLINSHEAD**
Printed and bound in Glasgae by Bell & Bain

Disclaimer:
The information contained in this *1314: The Battle of Bannockburn* (the
"Material") is believed to be accurate at the time of printing, but no
representation or warranty is given (express or implied) as to its accuracy,
completeness or correctness. The author and publisher do not accept any
liability whatsoever for any direct, indirect or consequential loss or damage
arising in any way from any use of or reliance on this Material for any purpose.

While every care has been taken to compile and check all the information in
this book, in a work of this complexity it is possible that mistakes and
omissions may have occurred. If you know of any corrections, alterations or
improvements, please contact the author or the publisher at the address above.

CONTENTS

PREFACE

23 and 24 June 2014 mark the 700th anniversary of the Battle of Bannockburn and this wee book has been written to commemorate what is one of the most momentous events in Scottish history. As with many battles it did not win the war – or even the wars of independence – but it marked a pivotal point in the career of Robert the Bruce, Robert I, king of Scots, and of the story of the kingdom of Scots. Up to June 1314, Robert I's reign had been categorised by questionable legitimacy, dubious motives, fluctuating military success and unreliable support. After Bannockburn, a battle that Robert had no particular desire, his confidence and authority increased. On a mid summer weekend on boggy land near Falkirk, Robert I's army of a small number of skilled knights, of archers equipped with less powerful bows and of minimally-trained foot soldiers managed to defeat the much larger, better trained and better equipped army of Edward II of England.

Victories against the odds are remembered for their wider and longer impact: Bannockburn is no exception. The victory enabled Robert to impose his authority on the Scots, some of whom were strongly opposed to him; to negotiate the return of his wife from captivity; to demonstrate to other international powers that he was a strong king and successful military leader; and to further undermine Edward II of England's already unpopular rule. Without it, Scotland may well have ultimately lost the wars; the Stewarts might not have succeeded to the Scottish – and later the English – crown through Robert's daughter; and Robin Williamson would not have been able to compose his famous song 'Flower of Scotland', which has become the de facto Scottish national anthem (the words of which either resonate more or are easier to remember than 'Scots Wha Hae' or 'Scotland the Brave'...)

This book gives an outline of events prior to 1314: the problems of settling a secure succession; the brief reign of John Balliol; the involvement of Edward I of England in Scottish affairs and his invasions; and the short but inspiring contribution of William Wallace.

The battle itself is described in detail; and its consequences and legacy, both in relation to Robert I's immediate situation, but also in the longer term, are also covered.

The SNP-led Scottish parliament perhaps opportunistically selected 2014 to hold the referendum on Scottish independence as Bannockburn may be one event in Scottish history about which even the most disinterested will have heard. But leaving aside politics, to commemorate the significance of the battle, and its legacy, is neither nationalistic nor parochial but an acknowledgement of its monumental importance to Scotland's story and how we got here today.

Joyce Miller
January 2014

ACKNOWLEDGMENTS

Maps by (©) Martin Coventry
Battle plans by (©) Duncan Jones
Photographs by (©) Martin Coventry, Dorothy Miller (Tower of London), Gordon Mason (Bothwell Castle) and The National Trust for Scotland (©) aerial view of Bannockburn battlefield and statue of Robert the Bruce, Bannockburn battlefield (page vi) and statue of Robert the Bruce and Stirling Castle, Bannockburn (page 53). Many thanks to Marcin Klimek and Laura Cheyne at The National Trust for Scotland.

Aerial view of Bannockburn battlefield

Statue of Robert the Bruce, Bannockburn battlefield

1. A Kingdom in Crisis

B Y 1286, THE KINGDOM OF SCOTS was a land linked by trade and by royal and noble marriage to Norway, England, Flanders and France – among others – and was ruled by a continuous line of MacMalcolm kings since 1058, descended from Malcolm (Canmore) III, King of Scots. The south and east were controlled by nobles and lords, many of whom were Anglo-Norman, at least in outlook if not in origin, who held their lands from the kings by feudal charter and paid their rent by providing or supporting military service. The north and west, including the Highlands and Hebrides, were still dominated by native clans and chiefs, who were a mixture of Gaelic, Pictish and Scandinavian bloodlines – and who at times disregarded the authority of the kings of Scots and acted independently.

The thirteenth-century landscape of Scotland was very different from today. Instead of great open stretches of fields, much of the countryside was untamed woodland, marsh or moor, with small areas of cultivated

Highlands of Scotland

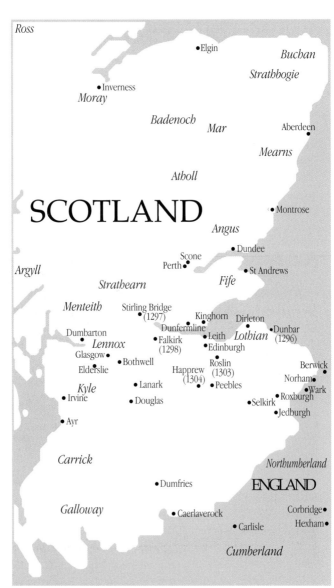

Ross

• Elgin

Buchan

Strathbogie

• Inverness

Moray

Badenoch

Mar

Aberdeen
•

Mearns

Atholl

SCOTLAND

• Montrose

Angus

• Dundee

Scone
•
Perth •

• St Andrews

Fife

Argyll

Strathearn

Menteith

Stirling Bridge
• (1297)

Kinghorn

Dirleton

Dumbarton

Dunfermline

• Leith

Lothian

• Dunbar
(1296)

Lennox

• Falkirk
(1298)

• Edinburgh

Glasgow •

• Bothwell

Roslin
(1303)

Berwick
•

Elderslie

Happrew
(1304)

Norham •

Kyle

• Lanark

• Peebles

• Wark

• Irvine

• Douglas

• Roxburgh

• Selkirk

• Jedburgh

• Ayr

Carrick

Northumberland

ENGLAND

• Dumfries

Galloway

• Caerlaverock

Corbridge •

Hexham •

• Carlisle

Cumberland

MAP 1: SCOTLAND: A KINGDOM IN CRISIS

land clustered around towns and villages. Rivers and lochs were generally broader and deeper, and in some areas more numerous. Much of the Highlands were still forested, and wolves and boar roamed freely, providing good hunting sport. Roads were few and often little more than tracks, so that transport by sea, loch or river was both quicker and easier.

By the reign of Alexander III, there were a number of towns, mostly located in the east and central lowlands, where the mercantile, commercial and administrative activities of the kingdom took place. The most successful towns had developed at key sites, such as Stirling, the

Stirling

gateway to the north with a royal castle and a bridge across the Forth; Edinburgh with a strong fortress and the nearby port of Leith; Berwick, Scotland's principal trading port and mint; and St Andrews, a major ecclesiastical centre and place of pilgrimage. There were other towns, such as Inverness, Perth, Dundee, Dunfermline, Dumfries, Roxburgh and Jedburgh, which grew and developed during the Golden Age of Alexander III.

The church was a hugely important international institution across the Christian world, with ties and loyalties throughout Europe and little regard for the concept of national boundaries. Scotland was no exception.

Up to 1472, Scotland had no archbishop, and the church in England, particularly the Archbishop of York, frequently claimed jurisdictional superiority over the bishops and church in Scotland. The Scottish bishops, however, were fiercely protective of their independence. They had been granted a Special Daughter relationship with the papacy, after the *Cum Universi*, a Papal Bull of Celestine III in 1192, so that the Scottish church was run by councils of bishops, independent of English control. The Scottish church would play a crucial part in Scotland's fight for freedom, while its close involvement and support for William Wallace and later Robert the Bruce, the future king, was as much about maintaining its own independence as that of the monarch or kingdom.

No medieval monarch could expect total obedience from his or her subjects. Across Europe, the great land-owning nobles were extremely powerful, with large numbers of followers in their own personal armies. Monarchs, most of whom were male, remained in power through a complicated, and often short-term, arrangement of alliances, family ties, and patronage. The main priority of the medieval nobleman was to gain, and then retain, property and land: this meant that nobles often put their own personal interests before those of their feudal lords, the kings. The situation in Scotland was further complicated by the fact that many nobles held lands in Scotland, in England, and even in France or Norway, and had to swear oaths of loyalty to more than one king.

Scotland and England had been on relatively good terms for most of the thirteenth century. After a bit of a difficult start, Alexander III's reign had been successful and, after the defeat of the Norwegians and their king, Haakon IV, at the battle of Largs in 1263, which led to the incorporation of the Hebrides into the kingdom, relatively peacefully. Alexander III, and his brother-in-law Edward I, king of England, were on friendly terms, and Scotland had prospered during the second half of the thirteenth century. A number of Scottish nobles had fought for Edward in Wales or against the rebellious English barons. Despite some awkward occasions, not least the Treaty of Falaise when William I, king of Scots, had been captured, Scotland and England were not the great enemies they were to become. Indeed, immediately prior to 1294, the two kingdoms co-existed in peace as neighbours and friends.

On 18 March 1286, a terrible storm hit the east coast of Scotland. Thomas the Rhymer would later claim that many predicted that its ferocity heralded some great disaster, such is often the case with alleged portents of doom.

Alexander III had outlived his first wife, Edward I's sister Margaret, and all his children; his last surviving son had died in 1284. His only direct heir was his young granddaughter Margaret, the Maid of Norway, daughter of Alexander's daughter, also called Margaret (who died in 1290 during childbirth), and Erik II, king of Norway. The infant Margaret had been recognized, somewhat reluctantly, by the Scottish political community as Alexander's heir presumptive.

Alexander had remarried and his second wife, Yolande of Dreux, was at the royal manor of Kinghorn in Fife. Alexander was impatient to leave Edinburgh and be with her to ensure the continuity of the dynasty, preferably through a male heir. A pregnancy the previous year had resulted in a stillbirth; but Yolande was young and clearly fertile.

Ignoring the advice of his courtiers, he crossed the Forth and set off along the cliffs of the Fife coast in darkness. Alexander did not reach Kinghorn and Yolande; on the morning of 19 March, the king was found dead, lying at the foot of a steep cliff, having broken his neck in the fall.

For 40 days the political community waited for any sign that Yolande might have been pregnant, but when it was confirmed that she was not, the political community – the bishops, abbots and priors, earls and barons – gathered at Scone to swear loyalty to the three-year-old queen in Norway. In her absence and because she was still a minor child, they elected six guardians, rather than one regent, who formed a provisional government to represent the young queen, the political community and the kingdom.

These guardians were Duncan, earl of Fife, and Alexander Comyn, earl of Buchan; Bishop William Fraser of St Andrews and Bishop Robert Wishart of Glasgow; and two barons, James Stewart and John Comyn, lord of Badenoch. These six formed a provisional government, often referred to as the Community of the Realm, and issued grants and legislation using a specially designed seal incorporating the figure of St Andrew and his cross.

Two of the country's leading nobles, Robert Bruce, (the competitor) lord of Annandale and grandfather of the future king, and John Balliol of

Galloway, had their own claims to the throne. In late 1286 Bruce, the competitor, and his son, Robert the Bruce's father, led an unsuccessful revolt in the south-west, in an attempt to press their claim to being Alexander's successor over Margaret. Neither Bruce nor Balliol was appointed as a guardian, but each had three guardians who nominally supported them, in order to maintain peace in the kingdom. The number of guardians was later reduced to four with the deaths of the earl of Fife and then of the earl of Buchan.

Of major importance to all those involved in planning Margaret's destiny was not just the question of her age but also her gender. As a female ruler, of whom there were few at this time, the choice of Margaret's future husband – to whom Margaret as a wife would naturally be subordinate – was key. Anxious to avoid any civil war, the Scottish parliament that met at Scone had sent three envoys, foolishly with hindsight, to Edward I of England to ask for his advice and protection.

Edward must have regarded this invitation as a great opportunity to extend the power and influence of his own royal house over Margaret and potentially over the kingdom of Scots. His son, Edward of Caernarvon, was just two years old, and a marriage between the heirs of Scotland and England must have seemed an obvious option. In any union, England would be the dominant partner in both size and wealth and, in any case, he could not risk allowing another royal house – France, for instance – to gain influence over the young queen and Scotland.

Edward's support was essential to the guardians, and calmed the volatile situation between the Bruce and Balliol/Comyn factions. Relative peace followed and the kingdom did not descend into civil war; however in 1289 Edward demanded that Margaret be given to him for safe keeping. He would ensure her safety and raise her at the English court. In November 1289 commissioners from Norway, England, and Scotland reached agreement at Salisbury.

The young queen was to be brought to Scotland within a year and was not to be married without Edward I's consent. Shortly after this, Edward I applied to the pope for a dispensation to allow a marriage between Margaret and Prince Edward, despite the fact that they were second cousins. The Scots accepted the terms of the treaty the following year in

1290 at Birgham. The treaty agreed to a marriage between Margaret and Prince Edward and to the creation of a union between Scotland and England. At the same time, the treaty appeared to guarantee to preserve Scotland as a separate, sovereign realm with its own rights, laws and liberties.

Edward, however, added some indications of English domination when he appointed Anthony Beck, the bishop of Durham, his viceroy in

Durham Cathedral

Scotland. In June 1290 an English force also seized the strategically important Scottish-held Isle of Man.

Despite these actions, the Scottish political community remained naively optimistic, and prepared for the royal marriage. The young queen Margaret set sail from Norway to Orkney in September 1290, but during the voyage she fell gravely ill. She then died, aged seven, apparently of natural causes, at Kirkwall in Orkney, leaving the succession to the Scottish throne wide open again and the realm in crisis once more.

At the news of Margaret's death, Robert Bruce of Annandale gathered together a strong force; at the same time John Balliol, now Lord of Galloway, declared himself heir to the kingdom. The civil war that the guardians had tried so hard to avoid now looked inevitable. William Fraser, bishop of St Andrews, wrote to Edward I, to request his help in naming Margaret's successor and preventing bloodshed.

Edward agreed to help but requested that the political community accept and acknowledge his role as overlord. This would mean that the kingdom of Scots would no longer be sovereign and independent. Alternative options were limited, so the guardians eventually conceded to Edward's demands, but added that their acceptance was only for the period of the interregnum – as soon as there was a new monarch the terms would be nullified. To ensure co-operation, Edward sent his representatives to occupy royal castles in Scotland, albeit allegedly as a temporary measure. He then sent out an invitation to the Scottish magnates and the various claimants to the Scottish throne, numbering 13 or 14, to come to Norham Castle in May 1291.

Norham Castle

Over the next 18 months, each of the candidates presented his claim, during what would be known as the Great Cause. Several claimants had very weak cases but still put their caps in the ring: the kingdom of Scots may not have been the largest or richest but it was still a respectable prize. The Bruce and the Balliol claims were the strongest; the others included John Comyn, lord of Badenoch; Patrick, earl of Dunbar; Erik II of Norway; Floris, count of Holland; John Hastings and Robert de Pinkeney; Edward even put himself forward as a potential claimant.

The English king declared that he would resolve the dispute, but not until the candidates recognised him as suzerain overlord of Scotland. After several weeks both the Bruce and Balliol claimants did so, although Balliol held out the longest. However, they followed the policy of the guardians and replied that they could not answer for the position of any future king but agreed, temporarily, to the English king's demands in order to enable a decision to be made.

After Norham, a court of 104 auditors was appointed: 24 by Edward, Balliol and Bruce appointed 40 each. Edward presided over the meetings at Berwick Castle. Six of the candidates were ruled illegitimate.

John Balliol's claim and that of the Bruces, came through descendants of Henry, son of David I, king of Scots, through Henry's youngest son, another David, earl of Huntingdon.

Balliol was the grandson of David's eldest daughter, another Margaret.

Robert Bruce, the competitor, claimed by the throne by nearness of degree – although he was descended from the earl David's second daughter, Isabel, he was David's grandson, while John Balliol was a great-grandson.

John Hastings was descended through David's youngest daughter, Ada, and Floris was a descendant of David's sister, another Ada.

Although there was no precedent for such a case, and the principles of inheritance were not firmly defined, on balance Balliol's claim was the strongest, based on the principle of primogeniture.

On 17 November 1292 John Balliol was declared to have won the argument and was chosen to be king. The majority of the Scottish political community supported the choice.

Civil war had been averted and the next king of Scots was to be John Balliol, King John I.

2. JOHN BALLIOL: TOOM TABARD

ROBERT BRUCE THE COMPETITOR had hoped his claim of nearness of degree would convince Edward I. Bruce also argued that he had been Alexander III's heir designate, possibly before the birth of any royal children. He tried to persuade the pope to support his position, although that may have been after it was clear that his claim would not be successful. Before the decision was announced formally, Bruce, the competitor, resigned his claim to the Scottish throne to his son, Robert Bruce, earl of Carrick. Carrick then resigned his title to his son, another Robert – usually known as Robert the Bruce – who would eventually become king of Scots. The Bruces went through these complicated legal arrangements in order to avoid having to acknowledge Balliol as their king and feudal lord for their lands in Scotland.

Prior to making his final decision, Edward consulted legal experts in Oxford, Cambridge and Paris. As well as the candidates, there were other key points which needed to be decided: firstly, was Scotland, and its king, a sovereign realm or, if not, could it be divided up amongst the different claimants? John Hastings was in favour of this latter proposal and during the summer of 1292, as it became clear the Balliol claim was regarded as the strongest, in a rearguard action, Bruce also supported this argument.

Although ultimately John Balliol was not one of Scotland's most successful monarchs, his short reign did ensure the survival of the kingdom as a larger and united entity. Had the Hastings and Bruce position been supported by Edward, the kingdom would have been broken into smaller, dependent regions which would have been under Edward's rule by the end of 1292.

As it was, John Balliol was inaugurated at Scone on St Andrew's Day, 30 November 1292, following the traditional ceremony of earlier Scottish kings. After six years without a monarch, Scotland was under the rule of an adult king. John, however, was in a different position to Alexander III: he had gained his title after a long, complicated legal debate, adjudicated by both Scots and English nobles and an English king. Subsequently, his

Scone

authority and relationship with both his Scottish nobles and fellow monarch was much compromised.

After Scone, John went to Newcastle and spent Christmas at Edward's court. During his visit, John gave homage to Edward I as his superior lord, and on 26 December, John knelt before Edward and swore: 'Lord Edward, lord superior of the realm of Scotland, I, John Balliol, king of Scots, become your liegeman for the whole realm of Scotland'. This ceremony was interpreted different ways. Some Scots saw it as a mere formality with no practical consequences; previous kings of Scots had participated in similar rituals; indeed the guardians and claimants had consented to the same terms during Norham and had agreed that any future king would decide about recognizing Edward's position as overlord on his own.

Edward of England, of course, had a different opinion about John and Scotland's position. It was unfortunate that in a time of crisis the Scots had looked to Edward I for help; although he had always presented a friendly face, he was one of the most ruthless and ambitious monarchs ever to sit on the English throne. One thirteenth-century English account described him as 'valiant as a lion, quick to attack the strongest, and fearing the onslaught of none. But if a lion in pride and ferocity, he is a leopard in fickleness and inconstancy, changing his word and promise, cloaking himself by pleasant speech. When he is cornered he promises whatever you wish but as soon as he is free he forgets his promise. The treachery or falsehood by which he is advanced he calls prudence; the path by which he attains his ends, however crooked, he calls straight; and whatever he likes he says is lawful'. This was the man who would soon become Scotland's greatest enemy.

After John swore homage at Newcastle, Edward renounced all assurances that had been made during the interregnum, and King John was persuaded to declare the terms of Birgham cancelled. In return Edward released the Isle of Man back to the Scots and cancelled some monetary dues owed to him. Then the English king displayed his full authority as supreme lord of Scotland: he began to hear appeals from the Scottish court in his own court. A number of Scottish nobles protested that Edward should uphold the earlier treaties of Salisbury and of Birgham that had appeared to guarantee the laws and customs of Scotland; this plea fell on deaf ears.

On John's return to Scotland he summoned a parliament to meet at Scone in February 1293. Most of the nobility and senior clergy attended, but the Bruces and some of their allies, including William Douglas and Angus of the Isles, were absent. Many of those who did attend, and had supported John's claim, expected to be rewarded: primarily, Bishop Fraser, the Comyns, and the MacDougalls; as well as several others. John's supporters were granted estates and responsibilities in the north and west.

Nevertheless John's doubtful authority over some of the powerful lords was illustrated by the MacDuff case. After the murder of Earl Duncan of Fife in 1289, Bishop Fraser had administered the business of the estates to the annoyance of MacDuff, the murdered earl's uncle. In 1292 MacDuff complained to Edward, and on Edward's orders MacDuff was permitted to recover the lands. As Fraser was one of King John's closest supporters, MacDuff was subsequently called to prove his case to the Scottish king and then imprisoned. When he was released, MacDuff again appealed to Edward and King John was called to appear before the English king in September 1293 to explain his treatment of MacDuff. John refused to answer on the grounds that he had authority within his own realm. However, under pressure from Edward, John yielded the point and agreed that Edward had the legal authority to decide the outcome of the appeal. Edward reinforced his point, by appointing one of his men to manage the earldom of Fife, as the earl was still a minor who was Edward's ward.

Although the case was to be heard in June 1294, it was postponed until the following year. Edward had other concerns: Philip IV of France had deprived the English king of his duchy of Aquitaine. Edward's primary concern at his parliament at Westminster in June 1294 was how to respond to Philip's actions, so he declared war on France and prepared a military retaliation. Scotland was to be part of his force and initially King John promised military support. A formal summons was issued to the Scottish king, 10 earls and 16 barons to raise their knights and men, and join Edward's forces in September 1294. War was expensive and many of the Scottish nobility resented Edward's demand that they were to support his campaign to reclaim his title of duke of Aquitaine. In September, Edward also had to contend with a rising in Wales, led by Madog ap Llywelyn, against similar demands from the Welsh to provide men and money for Edward's French campaign. Edward's departure for France was delayed, and it was not until March the following year that he was able to defeat the Welsh rebels. The Scots tried their own procrastinating strategies and appealed to the pope for permission to reject Edward's orders.

King John did not appear at the Westminster parliament in May 1295; in response Edward ordered John Warenne, earl of Surrey, and Anthony Beck, bishop of Durham, to travel to Scotland to persuade the Scottish king, and the argumentative Scots nobility, to obey his orders.

The Scots, however, had made a pre-emptive move and had contacted Philip of France, proposing an alliance between the Scots and the French. The Scottish parliament that met at Stirling agreed to negotiate a formal treaty with Philip, that was confirmed in October 1295. This also included a marriage contract between King John's son, Edward, and Philip's niece. The Scottish parliament, the political community of the nobility and clergy, had elected a council of twelve to govern the country. Although he was still king, John was declared incompetent to rule. This was an unprecedented move and showed the strength of desire from some of the Scottish political community for an independent kingdom, but it also reflected a level of contempt for King John's authority.

Not all of the political community, however, were willing to rebel against Edward of England. The Bruces, of course, were not prepared to defend John Balliol's position and fought with Edward, but others affirmed their loyalty to the English king under threat of loss of their lands in England.

Edward continued to issue summons for King John to appear to answer the MacDuff case and John continued to ignore them. Edward then led his army north, supported by the Bruces and the earl of Dunbar. The Scots issued a call to arms at Caddonlee, near Selkirk in the Borders, for 11 March 1296. After Easter, Edward I advanced up the eastern route to Berwick. The Scots ravaged south of the Border and tried to take Carlisle Castle, which was commanded by the Bruces, who managed to hold off the Scottish attack.

Edward of England ordered his forces to take Berwick with all possible force and speed, commanding that no lives were to be spared. The sack of Berwick was a cruel and savage act: not only were armed men killed but also women, children and the elderly summarily executed. The

Ruins of Berwick Castle (1905)

bloodshed was stopped only when – allegedly – Edward witnessed a woman being butchered as she gave birth. Berwick was the largest and richest of the Scottish royal burghs and, as such, its loss was a great blow.

The Scots' response was to ravage through Northumberland, burning churches and villages: one record described an unpleasant episode when 200 boys were burnt alive in their school at Corbridge.

Edward ordered Warenne to march to East Lothian and take the castle at Dunbar, which he did on 27 April. The siege lasted four days, during which time a force led by the earl of Buchan attacked the English. Legend claims that when the Scots in the castle saw Buchan's forces they cheered and raised their banners, taunting the English besiegers with the cry: 'Tailed dogs, we will cut your tails off!' – it was a widespread joke across medieval Europe that the English had tails. Unfortunately, despite their fictional tails, the English were more experienced in warfare than the Scots. They fell upon the poorly-organised and poorly-trained Scots and overwhelmed them in the first charge, sending them running back across the hills. Thousands of foot soldiers, unable to escape, were slaughtered and the earls of Ross, Menteith and Atholl were taken prisoner.

The following weeks saw little further resistance from the Scots. Edward took possession of the Scottish royal castles at Roxburgh, Jedburgh, Edinburgh, Stirling, Perth, Forfar, Aberdeen and Elgin, and many of the Scots nobles fell over themselves in their attempts to make peace with Edward and demonstrate their loyalty to the English king. King John showed little leadership; to all intents and purposes the Scottish parliament had already removed his authority, although he was still supported by a large contingent led by the Comyns.

John attempted to negotiate a personal peace with Edward, but his pleas were rejected. Edward demanded that John offer his total submission, renounce the French alliance and resign his kingship.

King John Balliol surrendered to Edward I at Montrose on 8 July 1296. His royal seal was broken and the arms of Scotland were ripped from his surcoat, hence the unfortunate nickname Toom Tabard or 'empty coat'. He was taken to London and imprisoned in the Tower of London.

Some Scots submitted to Edward and were appointed to administer the country, including James Stewart and Alexander, earl of Menteith.

Tower of London (see previous page)

For many, it seemed, loyalty and defence of the weak rule of John Balliol was less attractive than peace with Edward I of England.

After the seizure of Dunbar, Robert Bruce, the father of the later king, suggested to Edward that he could now claim the kingship of Scotland since John Balliol had been stripped of his title. Edward refused his request. By this point, Edward's position was that Scotland did not require a king, as he was its direct ruler. Indeed, Scotland was no longer a separate kingdom, merely a province of England.

In late July 1296 Edward progressed as far north as Elgin before returning south. To emphasise his total defeat of the Scottish kingdom, and its kingship, he seized the Holy Rood of St Margaret and the Stone of Destiny and sent them to Westminster Abbey. He held a parliament at Berwick Castle, with the dead reputedly unburied and rotting in the streets of the burgh, on 28 August where he organised his new Scottish administration and took oaths of fealty from almost all the landholders in Scotland. Over 1500 Scots recorded their names on the Ragman Roll, so called because of the many seals and ribbons attached to it.

Notable for their absence from the Ragman Roll are the names of William Wallace, his elder brother Malcolm, and his father. Edward's administration of Scotland was assigned to Englishmen: John Warenne, earl of Surrey, was lieutenant; Hugh Cressingham, treasurer; Sir Walter of Amersham, chancellor; and Sir William Ormesby, justiciar. Edward then turned his attention to the resumption of his war in France, believing that the Scots had been crushed. However, the administration he left in place lacked discipline and leadership: Warenne despised Scotland and returned to his estates in Yorkshire, leaving Cressingham to raise unpopular taxes from the Scots to help fund the French war.

Edward had exploited the rivalries and lack of agreement among the Scottish political community, despite the unity and loyalty to an independent kingship implied by the earlier declarations of the Community of the Realm. By 1296, ten years after the death of Alexander III, Scotland's king was in captivity and it appeared that the kingdom had lost its independence.

Coronation Chair, Westminster Abbey

3. WILLIAM WALLACE:
CHAMPION OF THE SCOTS

AFTER EDWARD LEFT SCOTLAND, an English administration took over many of the positions and responsibilities previously carried out by local men. These English men acted for the English king, who had removed a legitimate, albeit a rather weak, Scottish king, and who now demanded taxes and monies for his French campaign. Many Scots merchants and landowners were concerned by English plans to seize Scottish wool; Scottish churchmen were worried that English nominees would be appointed to positions in Scotland. There were also rumours that Scots would be sent to France to fight for Edward. As a result opposition gradually re-emerged. Two of the 1286 guardians remained in the country: Robert Wishart, bishop of Glasgow, and James Stewart, and these two men organised much of the early resistance.

By spring of 1297 there were reports from different areas about a number of clashes between English officials and local Scots. Two prominent leaders emerged: in the north, Andrew Murray, a noble whose lands and title had been seized by Edward; in the south, William Wallace, son of a landowning family, who had refused to swear an oath of fealty to Edward and was outlawed.

An earlier mention of a William Wallace recorded in an English court document of 1296, stated that, on 8 August that year, one Matthew of York, in the company of 'a thief, one William le Waleys', stole three shillings' worth of beer from a woman in Perth. Matthew, a cleric, was caught and sentenced to do penance for his crime; his co-accused remained free. It may be that this was not the William Wallace of later fame, as the name was not uncommon, but Wallace did know the area around Perth. The Wallace family held lands right across Scotland, from Ayrshire and Lanark in the south-west, to Moray in the north-east, and he would have been able to call on the help and support of kinsmen in order to avoid detention in a number of different areas.

Sir William Douglas and William Wallace led the revolt in the west.

Statue of Wallace, Edinburgh Castle

Douglas, as a lord, was a man of status and influence; Wallace was not and therefore his tactics were not those of a knight following the code of medieval warfare.

One story is that in May 1297 Wallace and a small group of men entered the burgh of Lanark and assembled by nightfall. Their prey was Heselrig, the English sheriff of Lanark, who is said to have cruelly murdered Wallace's wife. They approached his house, smashed down the door and killed Heselrig, his son, and his guards. According to Blind Harry or Harry the Minstrel in his fifteenth-century epic poem *The Wallace*, such was Wallace's fury that he hacked Heselrig's body to pieces before setting the building on fire. This act ignited further skirmishes against the English

19

in the south-west led by Douglas, Wallace, and other lesser men, who were part of the feudal network of James Stewart. Stewart had lost control of the south-west to the Englishman, Henry Percy of Alnwick, and as a result joined Robert Wishart, bishop of Glasgow, and the younger Robert Bruce, earl of Carrick, who all took up arms to defend 'the commune of our land'.

The death of Heselrig was a significant blow to the English administration. The position of sheriff was an important one: he was in charge of the collection of taxes and the enforcement of the law, and was also responsible for raising and leading the common army, the foot soldiers, who had always played a prominent role in Scotland's military campaigns. Across Scotland, the English sheriffs and other local officials were driven out.

The chronicler, John of Fordun, wrote, 'From that time there gathered to him [Wallace] all who were of a bitter heart and were weighed down beneath the burden of bondage under the intolerable rule of English domination, and he became their leader'. Many of the local uprisings may have been spontaneous; but there was an organising force behind the campaign: the Scottish Church. English chroniclers cited Robert Wishart, bishop of Glasgow, as troublemaker-in-chief: 'Not daring to break their pledge to the king, they caused a certain bloody man, William Wallace, formerly chief among the brigands of Scotland, to revolt against the king'.

After the raid at Lanark, Wallace's next target was Sir William Ormesby, Edward's justiciar in Scotland, who was based at Scone. The removal of Edward's justiciar would be a major triumph for Wallace, and the symbolism of a location such as Scone, the inauguration site of Scottish kings, would not have been lost on Edward or the Scots. The attack on Ormesby took place shortly after Heselrig's murder. Wallace and his men descended upon the English justiciar with such little warning that the he barely escaped with his life. He fled Scotland altogether, abandoning a great quantity of valuable loot, which the triumphant Scots eagerly seized.

Unfortunately the English responded quickly and the leadership of some of the Scottish lords was not entirely reliable. A force, led by Percy and Robert Clifford, confronted the Scottish lords at Irvine in June 1297, and another English force gathered at Roxburgh. At Irvine, Stewart, Wishart, and Bruce chose to attempt a negotiation with the English and by July, the nobles had agreed terms that allowed their men to disperse in return for promises that they would once more swear homage to Edward. Wishart and William Douglas were taken prisoner, having been identified as sacrificial scapegoats; Douglas's lands were forfeited to the English crown and he died in captivity a year later.

Once more it seemed the Scots had accepted peace on Edward's terms. Cressingham, the English treasurer in Scotland, took a different view however, and wrote to Edward's deputy treasurer in London: 'Not one of the sheriffs, bailiffs or officials of the Lord King appointed in Scotland can at this time raise a penny of the revenues of their lands, on account of a multitude of different perils which daily and continually threaten them'. Later he wrote to Edward, saying, 'By far the greater part of your counties in the Scottish kingdom are still not provided with keepers, because they have been killed, besieged or imprisoned, or have abandoned their bailiwicks and dare not go back. And in some shires the Scots have appointed and established bailiffs and officials'.

The leader in the north was Andrew Murray. Murray and his father had been taken prisoner at Dunbar, but the younger man had escaped from his imprisonment in Chester Castle and returned to his family lands in Moray. The Murrays, unlike Wallace, were rich and powerful, holding large areas of land from Inverness in the north-east to Bothwell in Lanarkshire. Many of their castles, however, had been taken by the English. On his arrival in the north-east, Andrew Murray raised the banner of revolt and proceeded to drive the English out from Inverness with the support of the local burgesses. Murray had strong connections to the church, as his uncle, David Murray, was a priest at Bothwell, a supporter of Scottish independence and later, in 1299, David was appointed bishop of Moray and Caithness.

Facing hostility from many of his own barons, Edward decided to release a number of the Scottish nobles captured at Dunbar, on the condition that they return to their Scottish lands and quell the disturbances there before they followed him overseas.

John Comyn, earl of Buchan, and John Comyn of Badenoch, were ordered to return to the north in the hope of defeating Murray. The Comyns met Murray near the River Spey in July but they did not attack; the high level of support that Murray had in the area influenced the Comyns' change of plan. The returning Scottish lords contented themselves by sending loyal messages of support to Edward, while they remained inactive and awaited developments.

After Irvine, many of the rest of the leading Scottish lords had decided to bide their time and returned to their own lands; they were reluctant to revolt against Edward again in case they were taken prisoner like Douglas, but they did not necessarily want to fight fellow Scots on Edward's behalf. At the same time, their men, the foot soldiers, joined Wallace and Murray, as also did MacDuff, earl of Fife, in the east. One English chronicler recorded that 'even when the magnates were with the king [Edward] in body, their hearts were far away from him'.

By August 1297 Edward was struggling to raise an English army to fight in Flanders and had to face challenges at Westminster about his French campaign. He eventually left for Flanders on 22 August confident that his knights and noblemen could be trusted to defeat the Scottish rebels. Warenne, as lieutenant, was ordered to return to Scotland but was reluctant to do so; this meant the remaining English garrisons in Scotland were poorly organised. With Edward's attention distracted in London and poor leadership in Scotland, Wallace and the other rebels were able to secure their positions, and it was not until September that a good-sized English force of cavalry and infantry marched from Berwick.

Murray and Wallace had joined forces and were positioned near the River Forth at the Abbey Craig, near Stirling, a mile north of the single bridge across the Forth. Between them and the Forth, ran the bridge, surrounded by marshy ground. Their army, made up almost entirely of foot soldiers, was greatly outnumbered by the English. Warenne had gathered a strong force, probably 600 cavalry and 20,000 infantry, many of them Welsh, to face a Scottish force of around 5,000 foot soldiers supported by possibly 150 horsemen.

Warenne, an experienced soldier, knew the power of his heavily-armed knights, and he assumed that their superior training and equipment would sweep away the common Scottish army. Joined by Cressingham,

Stirling Bridge, Abbey Craig and the National Wallace Monument

the English treasurer, the English army marched to Stirling. With its powerful castle, one of only a handful remaining in English hands, and its bridge crossing the Forth, Stirling was the key to the control of Scotland; the river formed a natural barrier through the east of the country.

Initially a parley was proposed. Warenne may have hoped that the Scots would surrender, as they had done at Irvine, and that would avoid any armed conflict; however Wallace and Murray refused. James Stewart, Malcolm, the earl of Lennox, and other Scottish nobles returned to the English camp and confessed their failure to Warenne. Perhaps as a token of their good faith, and more importantly to ally with what they probably saw as the winning side, they offered to join the English army the next day along with 40 knights, a promise they were not able to fulfil.

The English were ordered to cross the river the morning of 11 September and gather on the north side. The conventional wisdom of the day was that foot soldiers could not stand against mounted knights, no matter what the terrain; the knights' superiority came from their noble blood as much as from their arms, armour and training.

In order to cross the soft, marshy ground the heavy English cavalry would be forced to keep to the narrow bridge and causeway, where they could ride no more than two abreast. There, unable to launch their shattering charge, they would be vulnerable. There are reports that Warenne, accidentally or deliberately, slept in for the start of the advance, which caused confusion amongst the men and irritated Cressingham.

Following the tradition of medieval warfare, Warenne chose to create new knights prior to commencement of the battle, further delaying the start of proceedings. He then procrastinated even more and sent two Dominican friars to the Scots, to give them one final chance to surrender. The friars met with Murray and Wallace, and put Warenne's demand for surrender to them. Wallace reportedly replied, 'We are not here to make peace, but are ready to fight to defend ourselves and free our kingdom'.

Sir Richard Lundie, a Scot who had joined the English camp at Irvine, had seen the danger of crossing the bridge and causeway, and advised Warenne of the danger. He advised the English commander that there was a ford, Ford of Drip, quite near where more men could cross at a time. Lundie offered to take a number of foot soldiers and attack the Scots from behind, which would have allowed the rest of the English army to cross the bridge. Warenne and Cressingham declined to take up Lundie's offer and instead ordered the start of the crossing. Slowly, in twos, the English knights rode onto the bridge and along the narrow causeway. With banners and pennons, shining armour, colourful surcoats and horse-trappings, the knights must have made a vibrant display in the

Stirling Old Bridge

autumn sunshine. Meanwhile Murray, Wallace and their men watched and waited.

When the head of the English vanguard had almost reached firm ground, Murray and Wallace sounded the charge. They had split their forces into two: one group was to attack the leading ranks and the other to seize the north end of the bridge. The Scottish soldiers, armed for the most part only with 12-foot-long spears, swept down from the Abbey Craig and hurtled into the front of the English force, forcing them back onto the men following behind. More Scots soldiers ran down both sides of the causeway, stepping carefully across the marshy ground, and hacked away at the timbers of the bridge until it collapsed, plunging horses and

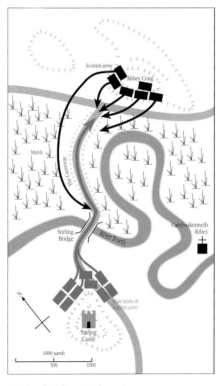

Battle of Stirling Bridge – 1

25

riders into the river below. Unable to defend themselves, the knights and their horses floundered in the marshy ground and were easy targets for the Scots. A body of Scottish spearmen, possibly commanded by Murray, quickly crossed the marsh and took the bridgehead, sealing the trap. The remainder of the English army watched the ensuing carnage from the southern bank, unable to help.

One English knight, Sir Marmaduke Tweng, managed to get free, and

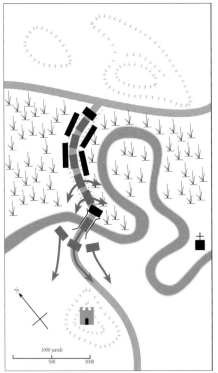

Battle of Stirling Bridge – 2

charge through the Scottish blockade to the bridge and safety. Many others were not so lucky: an unknown number of English and Welsh foot soldiers, and well over 100 knights, were slain, including the much-hated Cressingham; his body was flayed by the victorious Scots, and pieces of his skin were dispatched around the country, while Wallace himself took enough to make a new sword belt.

Warenne and the rest of his army fled; Stewart and Lennox, who had joined Warenne's forces before the battle, changed sides again and led the pursuit of the retreating English army.

Warenne and some remaining knights and lords managed to find safety at Berwick, but most of the English rank and file, foot soldiers, the wagon-teams and other camp followers, did not fare so well. They tried to make their escape towards Falkirk where Stewart and the other Scots lords were lying in wait with their men. As the vestiges of the English army passed, the Scottish nobles attacked. The English camp followers scattered, many were ridden down and killed, and the supplies taken as booty: medieval warfare was not always chivalrous and the acquisition of loot was an important part of any victory.

Stirling Bridge was a devastating defeat for the English. Although it was not, in the long term, a decisive victory for the Scots, it was the nature of the defeat that was so shocking. A mostly untrained Scots army had, humiliatingly, defeated an army of socially and militarily superior English knights; to the people of the time, such an event was unique.

The battle was won but the campaign was not over. During the following weeks English garrisons in lowland and central Scotland surrendered, leaving only Edinburgh, Roxburgh and Berwick in English hands.

In the immediate aftermath of the battle, there was much to be done. Only a month after the battle at Stirling, official letters were sent overseas proclaiming Scotland's independence. One surviving letter, sent to the

Site of Roxburgh

mayors and communes of Lübeck and Hamburg in Germany, informed them that their merchants could have 'safe access to all the parts of the realm of Scotland with their merchandise; for the realm of Scotland, thank God, has been recovered by war from the dominion of the English'. The letter was signed in the name of Andrew Murray and William Wallace, 'commanders of the army of the realm of Scotland, and the community of the same realm.' Despite the unusual circumstances, the forms, practices and business of the kingdom of Scots needed to continue.

Andrew Murray had been seriously wounded during the battle. Although both he and Wallace were appointed guardians and 'commanders of the army', by the November, unfortunately, Murray was dead. Wallace led forays into the north of England during October and November, looting supplies and forcing blackmail from poorly-defended northern towns and settlements. Some of these raids were savage and ferocious, the Scots killed, looted and burnt property indiscriminately.

Wallace's position, however, was unprecedented. As a non-knighted man of lower social status, his authority over the Scottish lords was weak. He had support from some of the nobles, notably Stewart and Lennox, and from the Scottish church, but it was by no means universal. One report noted that 'by force and by dint of his prowess [Wallace] brought all the magnates of Scotland under his sway whether they would or not'. Wallace's authority needed to be confirmed once Murray died, and he was knighted, possibly by Robert the Bruce, and named sole guardian during the winter of 1297/8. He was officially appointed to represent the interests of the realm and those of King John.

Wallace benefited from the significant splits that still divided the Scottish lords. Two powerful rival networks still exerted their influence over Scottish politics: the Comyns, related to the former king John Balliol and loyal to him; and the Bruces, still hoping their claim to the throne of Scotland would succeed. Wallace, at least for a while, represented a middle way in the defence of the kingdom. His military success, however, and control over the nobility would not last.

Edward and the English were shocked and outraged at Wallace and Murray's victory. The English barons and earls ceased their squabbling and made their peace with their king, and in January 1298, Philip IV of

France signed a truce with Edward I, abandoning the alliance with the Scots.

Edward was then able to return to England in March, determined to crush Wallace and those who supported him; he transferred his seat of government to York, and summoned a massive army to Roxburgh in late June, consisting of around 3,000 cavalry and 25,000 foot or infantry, many of whom were Welsh or Irish.

In early July, Edward's army started its march to Edinburgh. As the army advanced, they found the land deserted of both people and livestock: the inhabitants had fled, driving their cattle and sheep before them. Edward's army was too large to live off land which had been stripped of its animals and crops, so his men relied on supplies being transported by sea; when these were slow or did not appear, discipline suffered, particularly amongst the Welsh and Irish conscripts.

By 15 July the English army had reached Kirkliston, near Linlithgow, when, lacking provisions, the Welsh threatened to join the Scots. Edward had ordered wine to be issued to boost morale; unfortunately this resulted in drunken brawling between the Welsh and English soldiers.

With no knowledge of Wallace's whereabouts, the expedition was near collapse; indeed Edward considered retreating. Sir John FitzMarmaduke then arrived with news that the English supply ships had arrived at Leith and Patrick, earl of Dunbar and a prominent supporter of the English, brought news that Wallace and his men were camped only 13 miles away, near Falkirk. Suddenly the English morale lifted; the Welsh rejoined the army once their stomachs were full and Edward led his troops westwards.

As at Stirling Bridge, the English again had an overwhelming advantage in the number of cavalry; however at Falkirk there was no bridge or causeway to restrict their movements. Wallace could have retreated, but his troops, and particularly the nobles, were confident and impatient for an open field battle and he struggled to keep his authority over them.

Acknowledging that they would remain and fight with or without him, Wallace made the best preparations he could by choosing a strong defensive position. The Scottish army was positioned on the south-east slope of Slamman Hill; the front was protected by an area of marshy ground, the left by a steep valley, and the right by broken ground.

Wallace formed his foot soldiers into four schiltrons, close-packed circles of 1,000-2,000 men, armed with 12-foot-long spears. With the long spears planted firmly on the ground, their iron tips pointing up and outwards, these hedgehog-like formations presented a formidable barrier to charging horsemen. Between the schiltrons were the archers of Ettrick Forest, although with short bows they were no match for the range and power of the Welsh longbows. The small number of cavalry was positioned on the crest of the hill behind.

Despite Wallace's careful preparations, the battle on 22 July was a

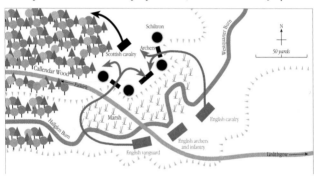

Battle of Falkirk – 1

disaster for the Scots. The left of the English cavalry, led by the earls of Norfolk, Lincoln and Hereford, charged almost immediately; the right of the cavalry, led by Beck, bishop of Durham, followed; the Ettrick archers

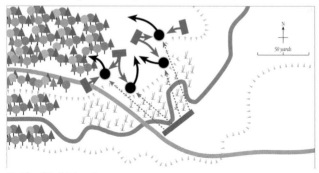

Battle of Falkirk – 2

were slaughtered and the Scots cavalry fled. But the schiltrons remained firm: again and again the knights charged, but could make no progress.

Edward then ordered the Welsh longbow-men to unleash a deadly rain of arrows. With men falling all around, the schiltrons began to fragment. The English knights continued to charge repeatedly, and the rain of arrows of the Welsh longbows eventually broke the schiltrons apart. Thousands of Scots were slaughtered.

Wallace himself barely escaped with his life, fleeing with a handful of men into the surrounding woodland. The Scots blamed their defeat on the divisions between different factions, and primarily on the Comyns and their supporters, who were accused of deserting the Scottish side at the start of the battle. Those nobles who died at Falkirk were not part of the Comyn network.

Edward, however, did not manage to consolidate his victory. He took Stirling, but supplies were still low and he was unable pursue the remnants of the Scottish army. He led his cavalry to Ayr in an attempt to capture Robert Bruce, but found only a burnt-out castle, already razed by Bruce. Unable to keep his army together, Edward returned to Carlisle on 8 September.

By burning his castle and retreating into the hills, the young Bruce demonstrated some of the tactics that he would employ to great success in later years.

The loss at Falkirk precipitated a change in approach by the Scots: in future they would avoid pitched battles as much as possible. It also meant the end of Wallace's time as guardian. He resigned his position soon after the battle, left the country and may have travelled on the Continent. Although little is known about Wallace's moves until his return to Scotland in 1302 and subsequent execution in 1305, he had inspired a new attitude among many of the nobles. Scotland was still in revolt against the English king, despite the defeat, and the English did not have enough troops for a full military occupation, so that only East Lothian was under their control.

Two new guardians were appointed towards the end of the year: Robert Bruce, earl of Carrick (the grandson of the competitor and future king, usually known as Robert the Bruce) and John Comyn of Badenoch, kinsman and supporter of John Balliol. They were part of the new generation of noble families; the sons and grandsons of those involved in the Great Cause, and their joint guardianship was an attempt to encourage the two factions to put personal rivalry aside for the good of the kingdom.

They were also able to call upon a wide range of support in several key regions of the kingdom. By August 1299, however, the uneasy relations between Bruce and Comyn began to break down. During a council at Peebles, a quarrel erupted: John Comyn seized Robert Bruce by the throat following accusations of treason, and the two men had to be separated. William Lamberton, who had been appointed bishop of St Andrews on the death of William Fraser, was regarded as a neutral influence, and was appointed as a third guardian.

For the time being the feud was patched up and by December 1299 they co-operated to prevent Edward's attempt to relieve the starving English garrison at Stirling; the capture of Stirling was a positive result.

The toxicity of the political factions within the political elite, however, was still a major problem; the rule of Scotland had still to be decided.

Stirling Castle (John Slezer, 1693)

4. Robert the Bruce: a King in Waiting

IN THE EARLY MONTHS OF 1300, the Scots were able to harass English forces in the south, particularly Galloway and Selkirk, but by May 1300 Robert the Bruce resigned his position as guardian, unable to work with Comyn. Bruce returned to his Carrick lands, and he remained there for the next two years. Comyn refused to co-operate with Lamberton and, to prevent Comyn dominating the guardianship, Sir Ingram Umfraville was appointed as Bruce's replacement. Umfraville was an ally of the Bruces.

By the summer of that year, Edward I had again managed to raise a sizeable army and he began his next campaign by besieging Caerlaverock Castle near Dumfries. The Scottish garrison asked for terms of surrender but Edward refused. The episode is described in the 14th-century poem *'Le Siege de Karlavreock'* written by a member of Edward's army. The English king was increasingly frustrated and angry with the continued Scottish resistance and he vented some of his fury at Caerlaverock,

Caerlaverock Castle

refusing the garrison honourable surrender terms. After his siege engines had made short work of the fortifications, several members of the garrison were hanged. This, however, was his only major success at this time, despite a number of skirmishes with the Scots who were led by the Comyns.

In the meantime, the Scots had been busy lobbying international support. Bishop Lamberton had appealed to Pope Boniface VII and Philip IV of France: Wallace may also have been involved in these diplomatic missions while he was abroad. Edward received a papal Bull that demanded he withdraw from Scotland. Outraged by this, but under pressure from Philip of France, he agreed a truce from October 1300 until May 1301.

Another important development was the emergence of John Balliol from captivity. In 1299 Edward had released Balliol to papal custody and, in 1301, he was transferred to his family estates in Picardy and given protection by the French king. Balliol also appointed his own guardian in Scotland, Sir John Soulis. Early in 1301, the other three guardians, unable to cooperate, resigned and Soulis replaced them as sole guardian.

The truce between Edward and the Scots ended in May 1301, and in July Edward embarked on another campaign, again into the south-west. His son, the future Edward II, marched up the west coast from Carlisle, while the king led the main army from Berwick in the east. The English managed to take Selkirk, Peebles, Bothwell and Turnberry, but Soulis was now in command of the Scottish resistance and prevented the English from advancing further north. Despite the divisions amongst the Scottish nobles, Edward was still not able to accomplish a decisive conquest.

Edward was again pressurised by Philip of France into signing another truce with the Scots in 1302. At the same time there was a lot of speculation that John Balliol was to be restored to the Scottish throne, accompanied by a French army. The possibility of Balliol's return threatened Bruce's position, and led him to change sides, so that he made his peace with Edward of England in February 1302. With his submission, Bruce secured his estates and married his second wife, Elizabeth de Burgh, daughter of the earl of Ulster, one of Edward's senior lords in Ireland.

The loss of Bruce and his army was a major blow, and the Scots also suffered from political developments in Europe. In July 1302, the Flemish defeated the French at Courtrai, and Philip was also involved in a dispute with the pope. In order to relieve some of the pressure, the French king agreed to a truce with Edward. In response, the Scots sent a strong delegation to Paris, including Soulis, Stewart, Umfraville, Buchan and Lamberton, to lobby the French king. Back in Scotland John Comyn resumed his role as guardian. The Paris mission failed and in May 1303 a peace was agreed between the English and the French; the Scots were left on their own.

Edward I was now free to concentrate on Scotland. The Scots had defeated an English force at Roslin in February 1303, but after the peace treaty with France was signed, Edward's well-prepared campaign began in Roxburgh and this time his target was the north: Comyn territory. He arrived at Elgin in September, having faced very little opposition during his progress north.

He then returned south to spend the winter at Dunfermline Abbey. The Scots were unable to offer any serious resistance, despite the return of William Wallace who, with Simon Fraser, carried out some raids on English garrisons in the south. Wallace was defeated at Happrew, west of Peebles, in February 1304. John Comyn and several other Scottish nobles,

Dunfermline Palace (John Slezer, 1693)

including the earls of Strathearn, Atholl and Menteith, but not John Soulis, submitted to Edward. Sir William Oliphant, commander of Stirling Castle, did not accept this surrender and subsequently Edward subjected the garrison to a three-month-long siege, during which time he tested every siege engine that he could find, including his Warwolf or *Loup de Guerre*. Even when the defenders finally offered their surrender on 24 July, Edward persisted for several more days, and, as at Caerlaverock, the surrendering garrison at Stirling was subjected to extremely harsh punishment.

As part of the Scottish submission, Edward demanded that William Wallace was to be handed over to the English: 'No words of peace are to be held out to William Wallace in any circumstances whatever unless he places himself utterly and absolutely in our will'.

Both English and some Scots pursued Wallace relentlessly, until he was finally captured, near Glasgow, in August 1305 by a spy in the pay of Sir John Menteith. He was taken to London with his legs tied beneath his horse. On 23 August a procession led him to Westminster Hall, where he was tried for his crimes against the English, which he admitted. He was also charged with treason against Edward I, which he denied, having never sworn homage to Edward as his king.

The trial was a mere formality, the judgement, and sentence, an inevitable conclusion. Wallace was taken to Smithfield Elms, where he was hanged, cut down, disembowelled and beheaded. His heart and entrails were burned, and his body was quartered, the four parts being sent to Newcastle, Berwick, Stirling and Perth; his head was displayed above London Bridge.

Other Scots who had refused to submit to Edward faced different options: Simon Fraser submitted but Soulis went into exile in France and died there five years later.

The Scots were once more under Edward's rule and Balliol was not going to return as king. Nevertheless, many of the Scots nobility had their lands and titles restored, and Comyn had managed to negotiate Edward's agreement that the laws and customs of Scotland as they had been in the reign of Alexander III should be maintained.

Over the next 18 months forfeited lands were returned. At Westminster in September 1305, Edward's Ordinance for the good order of Scotland was published; the administrators of Scotland were English, including Edward's nephew, John of Brittany, but 18 of the 22 sheriffs were to be Scots. Edward's policy was now more about co-operation than coercion.

The long years of campaigning in Wales, France and Scotland had taken their toll on the English king and his subjects. Edward was old, (he was 66) and in order to ensure what he hoped would be a lasting peace in Scotland, and remove any threat of further rebellion, he needed the support of a significant number of the Scottish nobles. He must have hoped this new policy would at long last bring an end to the fighting: it did not.

Statue of Wallace, National Wallace Monument

5. ROBERT I, KING OF SCOTS

I N FEBRUARY 1306, Edward's justiciars were at a session at Dumfries
Castle, Robert the Bruce was at Lochmaben having fled London, and
John Comyn was nearby at Dalswinton.

Bruce requested a meeting with Comyn, although it seems unlikely
that what ultimately happened at Dumfries was premeditated. The two
men, accompanied by their entourages, agreed to meet in early February
at the Franciscan friary, or Greyfriars, in Dumfries. The purpose may
have been reconciliation and the situation in Scotland, but at some point
– sources suggest – Robert accused Comyn of treachery, tempers flared
and they came to blows, much as they had done at Peebles in 1299. This
time it was far more serious: Bruce attacked Comyn with his sword and
Comyn was left for dead at the altar.

Some accounts claim that it was one of Bruce's companions who struck
the fatal blow rather than Bruce himself. Undoubtedly Bruce needed to
give this violent act a positive spin, as the consequences for a king were
serious: killing a man inside the confines of a church was a sacrilegious
act. Although the murder may not have been premeditated, the speed
with which Bruce and his supporters acted does indicate that a
contingency plan had already been considered.

Robert was officially Edward's enemy and the rest of the Comyns sought
revenge for the slaying of their leader. The garrison at Dumfries Castle
surrendered and Bruce then started his campaign to take control of the
south-west. He seized Ayr, followed by Dalswinton, Tibbers and Inverkip,
all properties of the Comyns or their supporters. Bruce's men also took
Rothesay and Dunaverty.

The English response was slow but it was not until Bruce went to
Glasgow to meet Bishop Wishart that he was able to declare his claim to
the throne. Wishart absolved him of his crime at Dumfries, and the
Scottish church rallied behind Bruce and his cause, leaving him free 'to
secure his heritage'. A formal notice was sent to Edward I that he should
recognise Robert the Bruce as king of Scots.

Bruce was at Scone by March 1306, where he was inaugurated

MAP 2: SCOTLAND: THE ROAD TO BANNOCKBURN

as Robert I, king of Scots. The bishops of Glasgow, St Andrews and Moray, and the earls of Atholl, Lennox and Menteith were at the ceremony. King Robert wore the kingly robes and vestments, and a circlet of gold was placed on his head, which act was traditionally carried out by the earl of Fife. The earl at that time was a minor and a ward of Edward I so his aunt, Isabella, countess of Buchan, took her nephew's place, despite being married to the Comyn, earl of Buchan.

Most of the rest of those who attended came from lands held by the new king and his key allies. Despite the help from Wishart and the Scottish church, Robert's seizure of the throne was not widely supported. Nevertheless, the king did not retreat to the safety of the south-west but was active in Perthshire, Aberdeenshire and Angus, where the Comyns had strong support.

When Edward I heard about Robert's revolt he was outraged. At the Feast of Pentecost, 22 May, he knighted his son, who in turn knighted all eligible squires. They all swore, on two swans enmeshed in gold chains, never to rest until Scotland was subdued. Prince Edward advanced towards Carlisle at the head of a large army; his ailing father followed behind. The English also petitioned the pope to have King Robert I excommunicated for his sacrilegious act in the church at Dumfries;

The previous month, the earl of Pembroke, Aymer de Valance, John Comyn's brother-in-law, had been instructed to march with Percy and Clifford against the rebel. They were to show no mercy to anyone associated with the revolt. Pembroke advanced north and was joined by many of the Comyn faction. He reached Perth unopposed early in June, capturing Bishop Wishart at Cupar Castle in Fife, while Bishop Lamberton surrendered at Kinross. They were imprisoned in England, their lives spared only because they were churchmen.

Robert the Bruce and his supporters arrived at Perth on 18 June 1306, where he challenged Pembroke to single combat. Pembroke agreed to fight the following morning. Robert then withdrew six miles to Methven, but the English attacked and routed the Scottish king's forces at dawn. Robert escaped, but his army suffered a heavy defeat. Many of his companions and followers were captured and brutally executed. In the wake of Pembroke's success, Prince Edward and his army ravaged the south of Scotland until all resistance had been crushed.

Robert and a few followers fled to the mountains but were defeated near Loch Tay and again at Dalry in Argyll. The MacDougall, lord of Lorn, a son-in-law of the dead Comyn, controlled this area, and wanted to revenge the death of his kinsman. The MacDougall clansmen hid at the entrance to the narrow pass at Dalry and, as the king's small force passed, MacDougall's men attacked down the slopes, slashing at the horses and riders with their axes. The king and a small number of his party, including James Douglas, managed to escape by retreating along a narrow track.

Following his defeat at Methven, Robert had ordered his wife Elizabeth and daughter Marjorie to travel north to Kildrummy for safety. They were accompanied by one of his brothers, Neil (or Nigel), and the earl of Atholl. When they reached Kildrummy, Pembroke was already at Aberdeen preparing to attack, so the royal ladies continued northward with Atholl. When the earl of Ross, a Comyn supporter, heard of their progress into Easter Ross, he decided to capture them. They tried to claim sanctuary at the chapel of St Duthac at Tain, but were seized by the earl of Ross and sent south to Lanercost Priory in England.

After the fall of Kildrummy Castle, Neil Bruce was also captured. The siege was ended by the treachery of the castle blacksmith when he set

Kildrummy Castle

fire to the corn store in return for English gold. The flames quickly spread to the castle gate, and the English were able to gain entry. After a day of fighting the defenders surrendered. The blacksmith was rewarded with his gold; allegedly it was poured molten down his throat. Edward I was ruthless. The prisoners were deemed traitors: Neil Bruce, Atholl, and Simon Fraser were hanged and beheaded.

Robert the Bruce's womenfolk, including his wife, daughter and sisters, were spared execution but were imprisoned in harsh conditions. His sister Mary Bruce and Isabella, countess of Buchan, who had crowned him, spent the next four years in cages suspended from the battlements of Roxburgh and Berwick castles. Marjorie and Christina Bruce were sent to convents, and Robert's wife Elizabeth was held under house arrest at Burstwick-in-Holderness for eight years.

Robert hoped to reach the safe territory of his supporters in Lennox and Cowal, but the English, helped by Sir John Menteith, pursued the king to the west. From Kintyre, Robert headed to the Hebrides and he may have spent the following five or six months in the isles, possibly including Rathlin, off the north coast of Ireland.

The MacDonalds of Islay and MacRuaries of Garmoran, old enemies of the MacDougalls, offered Robert protection during these difficult winter months. Their support of Robert at this time was crucial. He was able to make plans and gain support free from fear of attack, while his brothers recruited help from the Ulster Irish. By the time Robert planned his return in the spring of 1307, he had acquired a fleet of galleys and hundreds of men.

The next stage of the war again did not all go well. Two more of his brothers, Alexander and Thomas, were defeated in Galloway in February 1307 by the MacDowalls, and executed at Carlisle on Edward's orders. Robert travelled via Arran to Carrick and managed to attack the English garrison at Turnberry, despite being tricked into landing when it was not safe. Robert disappeared with his men into the hills of Carrick, eluding capture and betrayal but realising that he could never defeat his enemies using pitched battles and chivalric challenges. Guile, cunning and knowledge of the terrain would be needed to fight a guerilla war. Although much of Galloway and Ayrshire was occupied by English troops led by

Pembroke, followers slowly found their way to the new Scottish king, and from the hills Robert and his men managed to harass his enemies and avoid capture.

On one notable occasion, James Douglas took a party of men to Douglasdale where Sir Robert Clifford held Douglas's castle. When the English marched to church, Douglas and his men attacked and took them prisoner. They then took food and supplies, beheaded the prisoners and stuffed them into the vaults, fouled the water supply, and set the castle on fire: the event was later remembered ironically as Douglas's Larder.

Robert had made camp at Glen Trool and in April, Pembroke sent 1,500 men to ambush the Scots. They approached the camp through woods, sending a woman to spy on the numbers of men who were with Robert. The woman lost her nerve and warned the Scots, who numbered around 300. The Scots just managed to arm themselves before the English attacked. Robert managed to fire an arrow through their leader's throat, and the English pulled up abruptly; the Scots were then able to advance and the English fled.

The defeat was so shameful that Pembroke retired to Carlisle in disgust. The news of Robert I's surprise victory spread, and encouraged more men to join him. Confident enough to leave the hills, Robert moved his army to Galston, near the English-held castle at Ayr. James Douglas, Alexander Lindsay, and Robert Boyd all managed to bring more local men to support the Scottish king.

From his sickbed, Edward I ordered Pembroke to reassemble his troops and advance to Galston, so Robert withdrew to Loudoun Hill. When the 3,000-strong English army approached on the morning of 10 May, Robert positioned spearmen behind ditches. When the first English squadron advanced they tried to avoid the ditches but fell into disarray and were driven back. Those not killed or unhorsed collided with the second English unit who had followed behind. The Scots then advanced steadily, routing Pembroke and his army, who fled to Bothwell Castle.

The victory at Loudoun did not secure Robert's position in Scotland but it was nevertheless an important event. Against the odds, the beleaguered Scottish king had won a field battle. Edward I took the news of the defeat at Loudoun Hill badly – perhaps his power was finally

Bothwell Castle

weakening. Reports were received in England that Robert 'had the goodwill of his people', and support for Robert I, king of Scots, was increasing. Edward summoned troops to once again assemble at Carlisle and rode at their head. The effort was too much for him.

Edward I of England, the Hammer of the Scots, died at the village of Burgh-on-Sands, near Carlisle, looking over the Solway to Scotland, the kingdom that he had never fully conquered.

Edward's final wish was that his bones be carried at the head of his army into Scotland until the country was fully subdued, but Edward II left his father's corpse at Waltham Abbey and marched to Cumnock, near Ayr. The new king, however, had returned to England by September and it would be some years before he returned to Scotland, distracted by his more pressing problems at home.

Robert I used this time to build up a tight, well-organised, group of supporters, which he was able to use to confront his Scottish enemies, firstly the MacDowalls of Galloway.

Dugald MacDowall had been responsible for the capture and killing of two of the king's brothers, Thomas and Alexander, and as punishment Robert exacted a bloody campaign of revenge. Many of Robert's enemies fled from Galloway to Cumbria; those who remained were given the choice of paying tribute to the new king or death. Robert then turned his attention further north and the MacDougalls of Lorn; David, earl of Atholl; William, earl of Ross; and John Comyn, earl of Buchan.

In the autumn of 1307, Robert advanced east through the Great Glen, capturing and destroying Inverlochy and Urquhart castles. The Bishop of Moray raised the men of Moray for the king and Inverness Castle was taken and slighted.

In October 1307 Robert persuaded the earl of Ross to accept a truce, and this enabled him to attack the Comyns in the east. The king's forces faced Buchan at Inverurie in May 1308. Robert had been ill beforehand but rallied enough to lead his men to defeat his enemy. Then, during the following months, Buchan was repeatedly pillaged and wasted by Robert's forces; the Hership of Buchan as it is known, forcing his enemies to accept him as king or be driven out or slain.

After this Robert was able to launch a similar attack on the MacDougalls. By mid-August he had reached the Pass of Brander in Argyll, a narrow glen between Ben Cruachan and Loch Awe, the main route to MacDougall territory. John of Lorn had set an ambush by placing his men above the Pass, but Robert was prepared for this; he had sent Douglas with a force of Highlanders to a position higher than Lorn's men.

When the MacDougalls started their attack, Douglas and his men fired arrows into them from above. The king's forces then attacked from below. Taken by surprise and unable to defend their position, Lorn's men made for the single crossing of the River Awe, and there they tried to destroy the bridge, but Robert's men captured it and advanced into MacDougall lands. John of Lorn's father surrendered Dunstaffnage Castle and was taken hostage, John himself escaped to England.

After Robert's successes against the MacDowalls, the earl of Buchan and the MacDougalls, the earl of Ross now decided pragmatism was a better option and he surrendered in October and swore allegiance to Robert. James Stewart and Thomas Randolph also submitted, and would provide important support for Robert in the following years.

Robert I, king of Scots, was then able to hold his first parliament at St Andrews on 16 March 1309, the first free parliament convened by an adult king in Scotland since the reign of Alexander III. The earls, church

St Andrews Cathedral

and representatives of the burghs were represented, but only a minority attended. One of the purposes of the parliament was to draft a reply to a letter from Philip IV of France. The French king had asked for the assistance of the Scots in a holy crusade, knowing that this would prevent Robert from pursuing war with England. Philip had also written to Edward II, his son-in-law, brokering a truce with the Scots that would mean that Edward could deal with his problems with his nobles. Edward II's nobles resented the relationship between Piers Gaveston and the king, and at their insistence Gaveston was banished to Ireland in 1308.

Despite the reasoning behind Philip's letter, it was still important to Robert that his sovereignty had been recognised by the most important monarch in Europe. The nobles and clergy of Scotland then made declarations that Robert the Bruce was the true heir to Alexander III, recognising Robert as their 'lawful and true prince'. The Declaration of the Clergy justified Robert's kingship, blackened the reputation of John Balliol, and accused Edward I of cruelty and violence.

Edward II of England, however, was not prepared to acknowledge Robert's sovereignty, and his attempts to negotiate a peace failed, as Bruce would accept no less. Edward set in motion plans for a full-scale invasion, prompted by repeated requests for assistance from areas in Scotland that were still held by the English: Stirling, Perth, Dundee, Bothwell and most of the Lothians. Robert ordered sustained attacks on these areas: raids, plundering, extraction of blackmail. The objective was to demonstrate that Edward II was unable to protect the inhabitants of these areas.

In the autumn of 1309, two English armies were sent north, but there was little appeal in a winter campaign and a truce was agreed until June 1310. Edward then assembled a sizable force at Berwick on 8 September 1310, while ships were ordered to bring provisions up the east coast. For the next six weeks the English army marched throughout southern Scotland, but Robert and his men could not be found.

The Scots had been well warned, and Robert had withdrawn his army north of the Forth, leaving only raiding parties to harass the English. Running low on supplies, Edward II turned back to Berwick in late October and, at that point, Robert ordered his raiding parties to attack the retreating army with full force. When the English reached Berwick, Robert then invaded English-held Lothian; however by the time the English army had regrouped and returned to confront them, the Scots had once more disappeared north.

After this Robert started attacking Lothian and the borders with England repeatedly, and these raids lasted until summer of 1311.

England, however, descended into civil war, following the return of Piers Gaveston from Ireland, and Edward II had more to worry about that just the Scots. The Ordinances of 1311, criticisms about Edward's policies, were drawn up by 21 of his leading magnates, known as the Lords Ordainers. Edward was eventually forced to accept their demands.

Taking advantage of the instability in England, Robert called a parliament at Ayr in July 1312, and there he decided on a larger invasion of England. Crossing the Solway, Robert's troops raided from Lanercost

Durham

Priory, near Carlisle, to Durham and Hartlepool, plundering and taking prisoners. The inhabitants of Durham offered £2,000 for a truce until Midsummer 1313, but Robert also insisted that the Scots be granted free access through the county of Durham to enable them to raid further south. Northumberland quickly paid for the same truce, while Westmoreland and Cumberland gave the sons of their chief lords as hostages.

Galloway was finally subjugated when Dumfries was captured by Edward Bruce, another brother of Robert, in February 1313, by when Caerlaverock and Buittle had already fallen.

Robert had dramatically stormed Perth the previous month. The king of Scots had appeared to withdraw his men from the castle to a nearby wood, where they waited for a week. The Scots had found a place where they could cross the wet moat, and during the night of 7 January, once the garrison had stood down, they returned, waded through the moat and scaled the ramparts. Robert himself led the assault. By dawn the surprised defenders had surrendered, and the castle and town were burned to the ground on the king's orders.

The strategically essential Stirling, however, had to be taken at some point and, after his success at Dumfries, Edward Bruce was put in charge of laying siege to the strong castle.

6. All Roads Lead to Bannockburn

T HE BATTLE OF BANNOCKBURN would not have been fought if it had not been for the rash and romantic actions of Edward Bruce, the king's brother. In the spring of 1314, frustrated by the lack of progress of his siege of Stirling Castle, Edward Bruce struck a deal with Sir Philip Mowbray, the English warden of the castle. If the garrison was not relieved by noon on Midsummer's Day, it would surrender to the Scots. This was a bold move but, although such agreements were not uncommon, Edward's deal with Mowbray was definitely not part of Robert's strategy. As king, he would have to honour the bargain, and he must have known that Edward II could not ignore such a challenge; however a field battle was exactly what Robert did not need or want. It was a deviation from his preferred, and very successful, tactics of guerrilla warfare and covert assault – and was unnecessarily risky given the size and abilities of his Scottish force.

Stirling Castle

In fact, the agreement provided a welcome distraction from Edward II's problems with his rebellious Ordainers and came at a time when the English king had managed to reassert his authority. In October 1313 Edward had settled with his opponents: he had been granted a tax and had agreed that revenues from Gascony would be assigned to the pope in return for a settlement of £25,000. Ireland and Wales had been pacified, English relations with France were cordial, and Edward II was ready and able to turn his attention and military might against the Scots. In December Edward II issued a call to arms. The English host was ordered to be at Berwick by 10 June 1314; Edward II intended to lead his army into the heart of the king of Scots' territory.

At the same time, the Scots had not been idle and continued their raids on English-held strongholds. A Scottish attack on Berwick in December 1312 had failed when a barking dog alerted the garrison, but other raids were more successful. Linlithgow was attacked and taken between August 1313 and early 1314, when William Binnock used his hay waggon, concealing a small group of armed men, to prevent the castle gate from being shut. This allowed the rest of the Scots to enter the castle and defeat the garrison

During the early months of 1314, Thomas Randolph laid siege to Edinburgh Castle and James Douglas led a force through Lothian towards Roxburgh, initially harassing the garrison from his base in the surrounding forest. Douglas eventually took Roxburgh on 17 February 1314, Shrove Tuesday. While the garrison was enjoying their pre-Easter feast, Douglas and 60 men, disguised in black cloaks, scaled the walls using rope ladders. With no alarm raised, Douglas and his followers either killed or captured the surprised and unprepared garrison.

Shortly afterwards, on 14 March 1314, Thomas Randolph took Edinburgh. After many weeks of siege, Randolph had offered a reward to anyone who would lead his men up the castle rock. William Francis had lived in the castle when he was younger and was prepared to take Randolph and a small group; the rest of Randolph's men were ordered to assault the gate when the signal was given from within the castle. Randolph and a group of 30 climbed up the rock at night and, using ropes, they scaled the walls into the castle. After some fierce resistance,

Edinburgh Castle

Randolph managed to kill the constable and open the gate; the surviving garrison surrendered.

The taking of these important strongholds was a major success for Robert. It raised the confidence of the Scottish king and his cause: men came over to Robert's side, reducing the number supporting Edward. Following Robert's standard policy, most castles were razed to prevent them falling back into English hands and being used as bases for Edward II's forces. It also meant Robert avoided the costs and manpower associated with maintaining them as garrisons.

Nevertheless, despite Robert's successes, Edward II continued his preparations for war: he ordered 10,000 infantry from the north and Midlands, 3,000 archers from Wales, and organised the provision of over 200 carts and wagons in March 1314. More than 2,500 mounted knights, heavily armed and armoured, arrived and brought more mounted men-at-arms. Fully assembled, the English army numbered over 20,000 men, well equipped and ready for battle. Edward summoned support from the Irish, organised by Theobald Verdon, justiciar of Ireland. John MacDougall of Lorn, Robert's old enemy, also supported Edward II, bringing men from Argyll with him. There were other Scots, including

51

Ingram Umfraville, the earl of Angus, and Sir John Comyn of Badenoch, son of the Comyn killed by Robert, on Edward's side. The English army also consisted of men from Gascony, France and Brittany. Aymer Valence, the earl of Pembroke, was sent north as keeper of Scotland and Humphrey Bohun, the earl of Hereford, was ready with a large contingent. The English king announced he would be at Newcastle by Easter; however Edward did not have universal support for his campaign. He had not summoned parliament to obtain full official consent, which the Ordinances of 1311 had ordered, and so some of his most powerful magnates, including the earl of Lancaster, refused to attend.

By the beginning of May 1314, Robert established his headquarters near Stirling, ending all other military campaigns in order to concentrate all his attention and resources in preparation for the English attack to relieve Stirling. He summoned fighting men from across the kingdom and also ordered that any Scots who were in allegiance with England were to submit to him within one year or face forfeiture. Robert had gathered supplies to feed and equip his forces during his raids into northern counties of England and began to train his army. Estimates have suggested that a general summons throughout the Scottish kingdom at this time could muster only around 10,000 men, while Robert's force at Bannockburn was between 3,500 and 6,000, much smaller and less well-equipped than Edward's.

But Robert trained his men and chose his captains well. The vanguard was about 500 strong and was commanded by Thomas Randolph; the second division was led by Edward Bruce and numbered around 1,000. The third division, roughly the same size as the second, was under the nominal command of the young Walter Stewart and his cousin, James Douglas, who was only 19. Then came the king's own division: 2,000 Highlanders, clansmen from the north and west under Angus Og MacDonald, as well as men from Bruce's own lands in Kyle and Carrick. Lastly came the Scottish cavalry: 500 light horse, commanded by the marischal, Sir Robert Keith. There was also a small company of archers from the Ettrick forest.

Apart from the cavalry, the Scottish soldiers were on foot. They were armed with 12-foot-long spears, the same type that had been successful at Stirling Bridge but failed at Falkirk, nearly 20 years before, as well as swords, dirks or daggers. They wore heavily padded armour, or perhaps chain mail if they had managed to loot it during previous fighting; most probably they had a steel helmet. The Scottish knights, lightly armed and armoured, could not match the weight or force of their English counterparts, but they were certainly faster and more manoeuvrable. The archers from the Ettrick forest were skilled, but their light, short bows made of yew were ineffective compared to the Welsh longbows. Arrows shot from a Welsh longbow could drive through an oak door or through the body of a fully armoured knight.

A key advantage Robert had was trust and reliability. Many of these men had fought along side the king for years, and his captains had shown their abilities and leadership on many occasions. As soon as new recruits arrived, they were trained and disciplined and made into as strong and reliable fighting units as they could be. Robert may not have chosen to fight a field battle at this particular time but, once it was inevitable, he prepared his army and his ground as well as he could.

The Battle of Bannockburn was nigh.

Statue of Robert the Bruce with Stirling Castle in distance, Bannockburn

7. THE BATTLE OF BANNOCKBURN

E DWARD MARCHED HIS ARMY from Berwick to Edinburgh, and arrived there on 19 or 20 June 1314. On being given information about Robert's position, he then ordered his army westwards towards Stirling and arrived at Falkirk by 22 June. But Midsummer was only two days later and the English army would have to move quickly if they were to arrive in time. When they arrived at Falkirk, they were tired and hungry and forced to camp on open ground, with steep banked burns on either side.

Since the relief of the garrison at Stirling was Edward II's objective, Robert's forces advanced on Sunday 23 June and mustered at the New Park, north of Falkirk, an area of forest between the River Carron and the Tor Burn, blocking Edward's progress.

SUNDAY 23 JUNE

G ENERATIONS OF HISTORIANS have tried to locate the specific site of the battle of Bannockburn, a task made difficult by the vast alteration in landscape around the area over the past 700 years: areas have been drained, woodland felled, communication routes and domestic and industrial buildings constructed. Contemporary, or near contemporary, accounts, both Scottish and English, are also imprecise or confused about names and terms.

All of which makes it challenging to understand the precise events that occurred on 23 and 24 June 1314.

What is not disputed is the location that Robert had selected was as good a site on which to fight as possible for the Scots, not least because he also prepared the ground well. The New Park was located across the main route to Stirling and was on top of a bank, below which was the flat Carse or Pows. This was an area of marshland, cut by meandering streams including the Bannock Burn: 'a foul, deep, marshy stream', which led to the broad River Forth. The English would not be able to cross the flat area without exposing themselves to the same kind of rout they had suffered at Stirling Bridge, especially as the Scots were positioned on higher ground. To the west was the forest, but the Scots had blocked the road by digging numerous ditches or 'pottis' on either side, and had spread caltrops, three pronged spikes used for disabling horses, along the way. These were 'a contrivance full of evils... formed for the feet of horses... so that they may not pass without disasters...'. Robert also planned to organise his men into banks of schiltrons or battles. If the English cavalry chose this direction they would be trapped. Whichever route they took, the English would not be able to pass easily.

Despite these well-organised preparations, Robert may still have wished to avoid a pitched battle. Given the vast difference in numbers, he must have had serious doubts about a favourable outcome.

Robert sent the small folk: camp followers consisting largely of wives, mothers and children, cooks and prostitutes, grooms, squires, labourers and servants, with the supply train to Coxet Hill to the west for safety, hidden by the wood. Men who had arrived too late to be integrated into the trained fighting units accompanied them, for protection and to be called as reserves if required.

The English possibly anticipated a night attack as Robert's army had moved down from the high ground of the New Park and his men progressed on foot. Barbour's account of the battle states that there were four divisions or 'bataillis' led by the king, his brother Edward, Thomas Randolph and Walter Stewart, the latter supported by James Douglas. English sources recorded a more traditional tripartite division: vanguard, main and rearguard. Thomas Randolph led the vanguard; the king commanded the rearguard; and his brother, the main division. Douglas and Stewart probably did not command a main division but were present at the battle. Robert Keith was in charge of the cavalry, and the earl of Moray was posted at St Ninian's Kirk.

After dinner on 23 June, Edward sent some 300 men, led by Sir Robert Clifford and Henry Beaumont, earl of Buchan, across the open field of the Carse. This may have been an attempt to outflank the Scots and cut off their escape route. Meanwhile, Edward's main division approached the New Park where Robert was positioned, but then stopped in order

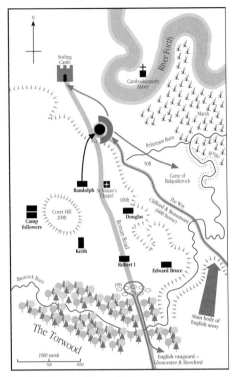

Battle of Bannockburn 23 June

to plan whether to set camp or to continue the march. The earls of Gloucester and Hereford, who commanded Edward's vanguard, continued the advance.

Their knights, eager for battle, saw the Scots across the valley, and assumed, wrongly, that they were withdrawing. The English crossed the burn, riding their horses through the water, weapons at the ready. Sir Henry Bohun, a nephew of the earl of Hereford, with a group of Welsh troops, dashed ahead to catch up with the Scots. In the woods he came upon Robert the Bruce, mounted on a small, sturdy pony. One English source recorded that Bohun tried to retreat but Barbour's version is a little different. Bohun couched his lance, spurred his warhorse and charged the king. Armed only with a battleaxe, Robert wheeled his horse round and rode towards the English knight. At the last moment, he swerved to his left, avoiding the lance; standing up in his stirrups, he smashed his axe into Bohun's face; he 'raucht him a dint', splitting his head open. Allegedly, the axe handle shattered with the force of the blow and Henry Bohun fell to the ground, dead: 'Bruce and de Bohun were fightin' for the croon; Bruce took up his battleaxe and knocked de Bohun doon'.

The rest of Bohun's men were overwhelmed and some tried to retreat, crashing into the following English vanguard, pursued by the Scots. In panic, many of the English fell into the hidden pits. The sudden charge had caught them by surprise, and a fierce melee ensued, although English fatalities and casualties were relatively few. The earl of Gloucester was thrown from his horse and only saved from death or capture by his squires. The English knights continued to retreat in confusion, with the Scots in pursuit, but they were called back by Robert.

The main advance division led by Clifford and Beaumont had moved towards St Ninian's Kirk from where they threatened to outflank the Scots. Randolph marshalled his men and quickly led them out onto the open ground, forming his men into the circular shape of a schiltron. Several English knights impaled themselves, and their horses, trying to break up the Scottish formation, but with little success. Douglas asked Robert for permission to go to Randolph's aid, but the king refused initially, however eventually Douglas was allowed to join Randolph. As Douglas and his men moved towards the fight, the English began to falter. The distraction allowed Randolph to seize his chance; he drove his men forward, drove through the knights and forced them to retreat or die. Some fled north to Stirling Castle, while others went south back towards the main body of the English army.

No further action took place that day. The English commanders decided to shelter for the night so they could prepare for the next day's action. They had also to defend against any possible night attack, so many of Edward's troops remained awake, dressed and armed ready for action. The English may still have hoped that Robert would retreat, but the first day had brought some notable success for the Scots.

THE BATTLE OF BANNOCKBURN

For years, Robert had deliberately avoided pitched battles, but this was a great opportunity: a glorious victory on the battlefield would help confirm his authority and kingship. If he was to defeat the English, now was as good a time as any. He could capitalise on the fact that the English forces were tired and demoralised after two forced marches and two defeats, and the Scots had had their confidence boosted by their unexpected successes.

MONDAY 24 JUNE

After the short hours of nightfall, Monday 24 June, Midsummer and the Feast Day of St John, dawned around 4 am. Robert had gained some last minute intelligence during the night: Sir Alexander Seton had defected from the English side and provided details about the lack of morale and general fatigue in Edward II's army. As a result, the Scottish king decided to commit to open battle.

The English had moved onto the dry but narrow ground, having crossed the Bannock Burn; the space was too constricted for the English army to spread out fully.

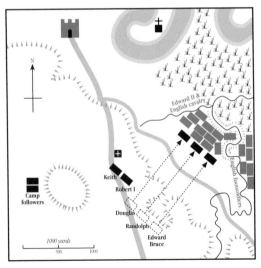

Battle of Bannockburn 24 June – 1

At first light, Robert and the Scots moved out from the shelter of the trees of the New Park and the Scottish troops ate a light meal as befitted a holy day

Robert made speech to his men, according to Barbour, citing St Andrew, John the Baptist, and Thomas Beckett. While the words that Robert used may not be those written by Barbour, it is likely that he used as much rhetoric as possible to encourage his men that their fight, and potential death, was for a worthy cause. As was usual, before such an important symbolic event as a pitched battle, the king of Scots knighted some of his supporters, including James Douglas and Walter Stewart.

The Scottish forces were drawn up in three schiltrons, and presented a dense bank of spears towards the enemy. Edward Bruce commanded the leading division, and marched towards the English positions, his right flank protected by the Bannock Burn. On the left was Thomas Randolph and a little further back James Douglas. Robert and his division remained with the Scottish cavalry, in reserve, on the slopes of the hill. The English were taken by surprise by this tactic: they had not expected Robert would risk sending the majority of his army out into the open field where they could be charged by the larger numbers of English cavalry.

The Scottish advance was temporarily halted when the Abbot of Inchaffray led mass and blessed the Scots as they knelt in prayer. Abbot Bernard de Linton of Arbroath carried the Brecbennoch, also known as the Monymusk Reliquary, which held the relics of St Columba. On seeing this, Edward II is reputed to have asked if the Scots were asking for mercy. Sir Ingram Umfraville, a Balliol supporter fighting for Edward, is said to have replied: 'They ask for mercy, but not from you. They ask God for mercy for their sins. I'll tell you something for a fact, that yon men will win all or die. None will flee for fear of death'.

Edward's military commanders, Gloucester and Hereford, were divided by recriminations over their poor performance the previous day. Gloucester then led an uncoordinated and poorly-supported dash forward, resulting in his death, impaled on Scottish spears. Many of the rest of the English vanguard suffered the same fate. The remaining English troops were crammed together on the narrow space of the ground and

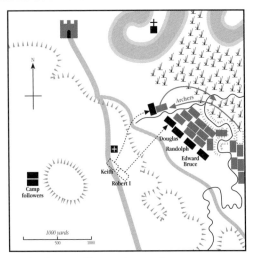

Battle of Bannockburn 24 June – 2

were restricted both in their ability to advance and to use the full force of their equipment. Once the English vanguard was broken, they fled in confusion back to the main body of the cavalry; panicking and often riderless horses prevented the rest from forming a cohesive force. The English vanguard had been reduced to a confused mass of men and horses, trapped by two stretches of water as the Scots continued their steady advance.

Unable to cross the streams, and blocked by their own cavalry, the English foot soldiers were unable to offer any assistance. Even the dreaded, skilled Welsh bowmen were unable to fire freely in case they hit their English allies. When they eventually moved into a position from where they could fire at Douglas and Randolph, Robert sent in Robert Keith with a small force of light cavalry who managed to cut down the unprotected archers. Although the English were being forced to fall back, they continued to fight strongly so Robert decided to send in the rest of his reserve, committing all his forces either to victory or to defeat.

As the chaos of the battle increased, not only was Edward II in danger of losing the day but he was also at risk of death or, more humiliatingly, capture. Accounts differ about whether Edward left the battlefield willingly

60

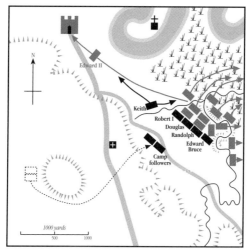

Battle of Bannockburn 24 June – 3

or not. Some versions state that he was led away against his will, while others are less sympathetic.

Whatever the truth, he fought his way across the burn and escaped north towards Stirling Castle. Barbour's account states that when the English king was seen heading away from the battle, the Scots shouted: 'On them! On them! They fail!'. The Scottish camp followers, carrying improvised banners and weaponry, emerged from behind Coxet Hill, cheering and shouting. At the sight of this noisy crowd, the will of the English army disintegrated further; their careful retreat became a headlong panic. The Scots captured many; others were crushed under the stampede or drowned in the Bannock Burn.

Once it was clear that the English had been defeated, the Scots were able to plunder their bodies and supplies: horses, armour, weapons, clothing, plate and food; one valuation calculated the booty was worth £200,000. Robert distributed the spoils amongst all his men; for most of the ordinary foot soldiers of Robert's army this was a welcome reward for their victory.

When Edward II arrived at Stirling, he was advised by Mowbray, the governor, that he would face capture if he sought refuge there. Edward turned south with Sir James Douglas in hot pursuit. Douglas only had 60 men but they caught up with the English king and his retinue at Linlithgow. The 500 English knights who accompanied Edward were too strong to be taken in battle, so Douglas contented himself with capturing or killing any stragglers. The Scots followed them so closely that, according to Barbour, the English knights had not even leisure to make water, and, reaching Dunbar, they abandoned their horses outside the castle gates rather than risk being captured. Earl Patrick allowed Edward access to

Bamburgh Castle

the castle, from where Edward, and a few trusted advisors, sailed south to Bamburgh. The remainder of his men were left to make their own way home. Many English and Welsh soldiers did not survive the journey, as they were attacked, captured and killed, and the ordinary folk of Scotland exacted harsh revenge in the weeks after the battle.

Edward Bruce was sent to capture other English nobles who had fled to Bothwell Castle; noble prisoners could be ransomed back to their families for sizeable sums of money or used to bargain for the release of Scots held in England. Robert was keen to demonstrate that he could act chivalrously and fairly, as well as command successful military campaigns. These hostages included many great and powerful English nobles, including Humphrey Bohun, earl of Hereford. For the return of Hereford, Robert was able to negotiate the return of his queen, Elizabeth de Burgh; his daughter Marjorie; his sister Christina; Robert Wishart, bishop of Glasgow, as well as 11 other friends and family members who had been held captive.

Boosted by their victory, the Scots were impatient for further action. In August 1314 Scottish troops, led by Edward Bruce, Sir James Douglas and John Soulis, raided through Northumberland, County Durham, Yorkshire and Cumberland, gathering booty and receiving tribute as they had done in previous years. These raids continued throughout the coming years, and the inhabitants of the northern counties of England suffered greatly and received minimal protection or help from Edward II.

In the end, the Battle of Bannockburn did not win the war or give Robert full recognition of his kingship, but it did help him to defeat his Scottish enemies. John Comyn, son of the Comyn killed at Greyfriars, was killed at the battle, and John Comyn, earl of Buchan, also died. Some of Robert's Scottish opponents were captured and submitted, including John Soulis and Ingram Umfraville. Others surrendered willingly: Sir Philip Mowbray voluntarily relinquished Stirling Castle and pledged his allegiance to Robert, as did Earl Patrick of Dunbar.

In November the parliament met at Cambuskenneth Abbey, near the site of his victory; at the meeting it was ordered that any landowner who did not do homage to King Robert would forfeit his lands. Most of his former enemies chose to become loyal subjects of the Scottish king, while those who did not were forfeited and became the Disinherited.

8. AT LAST, A KING TRIUMPHANT?

D URING DECEMBER 1314, Robert led an invasion into the Tyne Valley, which caused the local inhabitants to pay for a truce until June 1315. Another raid in early 1315 confirmed the demoralisation of the northern counties in England.

Robert was then free to develop another strategy to weaken Edward II's authority. In May 1315, he sent envoys, commanded by Edward Bruce and Thomas Randolph, to Ireland and offered to help them resist English domination. For many years the English had controlled Ireland, and men and resources used in the war against the Scots had been based at Dundalk, Dublin and Drogheda. A friendly force based in Ireland would give Robert a number of useful options: a strategic point from which to attack southern England; the potential creation of a joint force of Scots, Irish and Welsh; or the extension of the war with Edward II of England into new territory. It would also put some distance between himself and his brother, who had often acted impulsively, as illustrated by his challenge to Mowbray at Stirling. At parliament in April 1315, as Robert had no son, Edward Bruce had been named Robert's heir. If Edward died and had no sons, the throne would pass to Robert's daughter Marjorie and her heirs. Marjorie was married to Walter Stewart, which strengthened ties between the Bruce family and the Stewarts.

The O'Neills, the royal line of Ulster, responded to Robert's request; in return, Edward Bruce would be named king of Ireland. The Scots and Irish blockaded Carrickfergus, the main seat of the earl of Ulster; the earl was eventually defeated at Connor in September and Edward Bruce was crowned king of Ireland. This was a bold challenge to Edward II's authority and a distraction, which was exactly what Robert had intended.

Meanwhile back in Scotland, Robert continued to pursue his own campaign. He sailed to the Western Isles where John of Lorn had tried to gather support for the English king. Robert and Walter Stewart sailed up Loch Fyne; they laid trees across the narrow strip of land between East and West Tarbert, in order to avoid sailing all the way around the Mull of Kintyre. They then dragged their ships over the strip and crossed to the open sea. John of Lorn retired to England without support, and most of the men of the Isles rushed to give Robert their oaths of loyalty and assisted the king by harrying English coastal towns.

Things did not always go to plan, however. On 22 July Robert laid siege to Carlisle Castle and brought a siege engine with him, but the

Carlisle Castle (Francis Grose, 1783)

garrison of the castle had eight similar engines, and repelled the Scottish assault easily. On 30 July, Bruce tried a surprise attack on the eastern wall, but was defeated by the defending archers. Abandoning his siege equipment in the mud, Robert returned to Scotland.

In March 1316, Marjorie, the heavily pregnant daughter of the king, was thrown from her horse. Surgeons managed to deliver her child, named Robert, by Caesarean section, although Marjorie died shortly afterwards. The baby would eventually be crowned Robert II, king of Scots, in 1371, the first of the Stewart Kings, following the death of David II, King Robert's son, without legitimate issue.

Following a period of mourning, Robert turned his attentions to Ireland and his brother's campaign, which was not going very well. Randolph had brought news that Edward Bruce needed reinforcements. The Scottish king joined his brother in Ireland in early 1317 and they advanced on Limerick. Brian Ban O'Brien, an Irish chief from the south-west, had promised that the people of Munster would revolt when the Scots arrived, but instead Robert's force was opposed by Murrough O'Brien, Brian O'Brien's clan rival. Frustrated by clan feuds and hungry as a result of widespread famine, when word came that the new Lord Lieutenant of Ireland, Sir Roger Mortimer, was gathering troops to block his return to Ulster, Robert ordered a quick retreat. The journey north was miserable, through lands desolated by famine and plague, but eventually they arrived safely in Ulster. Bruce had to return to Scotland, but left many of his men with his brother. The king and Randolph sailed for Scotland, landing late in May 1317.

Following several failed English incursions into Scotland, Edward II had turned for help to the new pope, John XXII. Because of an interdict imposed following Robert's murder of Comyn at Dumfries, the Scots were not represented and the English envoys convinced John XXII that it was the stubbornness of the Scots and their refusal to make peace that had prevented the English from joining his crusade. The pope immediately demanded a two-year truce, and letters conveying this order were sent to the English and Scottish kings in the autumn of 1317.

The letter was delivered to Robert by two envoys, who he received with courtesy. The letter, however, was addressed to Robert Bruce, acting as king of Scots, so Robert returned the letter unopened. Another papal emissary was dispatched, but when Robert saw that the name had not been changed, he again refused to accept the letter. Following this, the envoy was attacked on the road to Berwick, and his clothes and documents stolen.

Berwick was an important burgh for both the Scots and the English during the medieval period. Robert had failed to capture it in December 1312 but decided to try again. Six years later in 1318, one of the local burgesses promised to let the Scots in, and Sir Robert Keith assembled his men, joined by Douglas and Randolph. On the night of 1 April, they crept to the wall and scaled it with ladders. The plan was they were to wait for the king's arrival, but Douglas and Randolph were not able to prevent their men from looting the town.

In the resultant panic, many of the townsfolk fled to the castle, and roused the garrison. Douglas and Randolph fought almost single-handedly until Robert arrived with reinforcements and the burgh was eventually secured. Within three months the castle was starved into surrendering. Robert did not destroy the stronghold, as was his usual strategy, but instead it was repaired and garrisoned. It was more important to control Berwick than leave it for the English to take back. Walter Stewart was left in command.

Bad news, however, followed this success. Edward Bruce's position in Ireland had remained weak: he only had control of Ulster and had not extended his support further south. Carrickfergus had finally surrendered but, in October 1318, when Bruce launched another invasion of Leinster, he was confronted with an Anglo-Irish force at Dundalk. Edward Bruce was abandoned by his Irish allies during the battle, and he and his close followers were killed. The English subsequently retook Carrickfergus.

With the death of Edward Bruce, Robert was deprived of his last remaining adult brother and, in the space of two years, both of the king's heirs had died. His two-year old grandson, Robert Stewart, was named as his new heir at a parliament held in December 1318. In the event of Robert Stewart succeeding while still a minor, Randolph was named as regent. Robert also ordered that conspirators against the king were to be imprisoned. Although Robert had achieved much over the past years, there were still those who opposed his authority and his heir was a vulnerable infant.

To compound Robert's anxieties, in June 1319, Edward II and Thomas, earl of Lancaster, mustered English forces at Newcastle and prepared to reclaim Berwick. The English army numbered around 12,000, and on their arrival at the town they formed a huge encampment around the walls. The assault started on 7 September, but the English were unable to break through and they withdrew to their camp. Five days later they launched another attack, from both land and sea, but despite heavy losses the Scots, led by Walter Stewart, again defended throughout the day.

The king of Scots was unable to relieve the town, but was aware that Edward II's queen, Isabella, was in York. Robert formed a bold plan to capture the queen and use her as a hostage to negotiate a peace.

A Scottish spy in York, however, was captured and revealed the plot. The archbishop of York made sure that Isabella was sent to Nottingham

York Minster

and then attacked the Scots. The improvised English army approached in great disarray and, as they advanced, the Scots set fire to grass, providing a smoke screen. The Scots then formed into a single schiltron and, as the smoke cleared, advanced. Most of the archbishop's men fled, but 300 were killed. The encounter became known as the Chapter of Mitton.

The Scots continued their advance through Yorkshire, burning and pillaging. Edward II did consider turning south to pursue the Scots but, under pressure from the southern nobles, chose to continue the siege of Berwick. As a result, the earl of Lancaster retreated in disgust, taking his troops with him, leaving Edward with a much-depleted army. The English king was forced to abandon the siege, and return south.

Once the English army disbanded in November, Douglas led a savage raid on Westmoreland and Cumberland, burning the harvest and taking hostages and livestock. Faced with the repeated failure of his armies and the continuous suffering of his northern subjects, Edward II opened negotiations with Robert for a truce.

Envoys met at Berwick, still held by the Scots, on 22 December 1319, where they negotiated terms for a two-year truce to start on 1 January 1320.

9. 'OUR MOST TIRELESS PRINCE, KING AND LORD; THE LORD ROBERT'

IN NOVEMBER 1319 the pope summoned Robert and four Scottish bishops to appear at Avignon. The letter did not acknowledge Robert as king of Scots, and again he refused to accept it. In retaliation, the pope ordered the English bishops to repeat the notices of excommunication against Bruce and also against the Scottish bishops.

Prompted by the pope's actions, letters were composed in the name of the king, Bishop Lamberton, the rest of the clergy and the nobles and freeholders. These letters presented the case for Robert's, and those of his subjects, legitimate actions. The letter of the barons, which is better known as the Declaration of Arbroath, survived, while the others did not. Several copies and versions of the barons' letter were made in later years and, while it has been somewhat inaccurately cited in modern times as an early example of democracy and freedom, its main purpose was to persuade the pope to lift the sentence of excommunication. Although its authorship is uncertain, the final version may have been completed at Arbroath by the Abbot Bernard de Linton, hence the name.

The letters were designed to present a united front, and this one carried the seals of eight earls and 31 barons. The rhetoric was emotive and the argument well organised. It described the rights of Scots as an ancient people, their unbroken line of native kings, the unfair attacks by Edward I on the people of Scotland and its church; and the timely and successful intervention of Robert I who had saved the people, the nation and the church, and who ruled by the assent of his subjects. The letter also contained a warning: if Robert made a peace with England that threatened the right and liberties of the people, they would reject him and 'drive him out as our enemy'.

All this sounds very dramatic but in reality it was just a petition and a piece of propaganda. Petitions to the papacy were not uncommon:

Edward I had sent pleading letters; Philip of France had also sent similar missives. The Scottish clergy had sent a petition in 1309-10 and the Irish Remonstrance had been dispatched in 1318, outlining Edward Bruce's case to be crowned king of Ireland.

The Declaration of Arbroath, therefore, was part of a longer tradition and, although a very sophisticated example, its rhetoric was not unique, and its claim of united support for Robert was overly ambitious.

In 1320, Robert survived another political crisis: a conspiracy to murder him was revealed. A group of former Balliol supporters, including some of the Disinherited and some of the signatories of the Declaration of Arbroath, had been encouraged by the appearance of Edward Balliol, son of the former king, in 1318. He fought along side Edward II at Berwick and for some the restoration of the Balliol line, even if it resulted in recognition of Edward II as overlord, meant they could recover their lost estates. But the plot was revealed, and the conspirators fled to England or were tried for treason. Soulis was imprisoned, some were executed, and others acquitted. Patrick, earl of Dunbar and Murdoch Menteith revealed the plot to Robert; Menteith was rewarded with an earldom.

At the end of 1321 Robert diverted his attention south to take advantage of the political instability and deterioration in relations between Edward II and his nobles. Another civil war threatened in England, caused by the king's new favourite, Hugh Despenser, who was opposed by Humphrey Bohun, earl of Hereford, and others, including the earl of Lancaster. Lancaster sought Scottish assistance to dethrone Edward II and conducted secret negotiations with Douglas and Randolph. Lancaster's proposal was that if Robert led an army into England Lancaster would support him.

When the two-year truce ended on 1 January 1322, Randolph, Douglas and Walter Stewart led renewed raids into England. The English northern lords were defenceless without Lancaster's help, who feigned an excuse for not helping them. Lancaster and Hereford joined forces at Burton-on-Trent, but the English king managed to drive them back. The earls retreated north, hoping to join up with the Scots, but were caught and defeated at Boroughbridge by Andrew Harclay, governor of Carlisle. Hereford was killed at the battle on 16 March, and Lancaster captured. Edward II ordered his execution without trial, quite possibly in revenge for his involvement in the death of Piers Gaveston, ten years earlier.

Renewal of the war was now Edward II's main objective, with the defeat of his English rebels, he was more confident that he could break the Scots by force and ordered his army to muster at Newcastle. In July, while the English army assembled in the east, Robert invaded English towns on the west, and spent the next three weeks plundering Cumberland, Lancaster and Preston. He then camped near Carlisle for five days, and used stolen cattle to trample and destroy the surrounding crops, before crossing back into Scotland on 24 July. By August Edward had assembled an army numbering around 20,000 and marched north to Lothian. He also ordered ships to attack the west coast, while others brought provisions to the Firth of Forth.

The main Scottish army was assembled north of the Forth. The Scottish king had ordered the evacuation of all the lands to the border, clearing it of people and animals, and burning all crops and dwellings. Edward II's army marched to Edinburgh through a devastated land. They waited at Edinburgh for the much-needed provision ships, but these were delayed by adverse weather. Men were sent into the countryside to forage for food, but could find little. By late September the starving English army was forced to withdraw. Robert, with a well-fed force at his disposal, invaded England again, crossing the Solway on 1 October and again harried Northumberland. He then advanced further south in order to force another battle and to capture Edward II. Edward managed to avoid capture but his troops were defeated at Byland in Yorkshire.

At Byland, Robert mounted a frontal assault on the narrow path up the hillside. Douglas and Randolph were ordered to lead the attack, but when their progress was slow, Robert ordered Highlanders to climb the cliffs to one side of the path and attack the English on their flank; when they reached the top, the Highlanders charged. The English were forced to fall back, then fled. Many knights were captured, but Edward II had received warning and escaped to York, abandoning his baggage and treasure. The earl of Richmond was imprisoned for two years until a ransom of £20,000 was paid. A number of French knights were also captured, but Robert ensured that they were treated with hospitality and returned without ransom. On 2 November the Scots went home.

Byland Abbey

Edward's travails were not over. His reputation had been further damaged by another failed campaign in Scotland and defeat at Byland, while his northern subjects continued to be harassed the Scots. Andrew Harclay, now earl of Carlisle, approached Robert on 3 January 1323. With the failure of the English king to defend his people or to come to peace with the Scots, Harclay negotiated a secret peace on his own initiative. The treaty allowed for both countries to be independent, each with their own king and laws. Harclay was in open defiance of the English king and Edward II was outraged by this treason, and the earl was captured and executed as a traitor.

Despite Harclay's execution, the rest of the English political community welcomed his proposals, and Edward II was forced to recognise the need to end hostilities. At Bishopthorpe, on 30 May 1323, the English signed a 13-year truce, which was ratified by Robert eight days later. The English agreed not to oppose Scottish attempts to have the papal interdict lifted, or to attack Scottish trading ships.

Thomas Randolph was given an audience with Pope John XXII at Avignon on New Year's Day 1324. Randolph explained that King Robert had been prevented from joining a crusade by a clerical error: the omission of his title from earlier papal communications. Once Randolph's appeal had been expressed in such careful diplomatic language, the pope agreed to rectify this and, finally, recognised Robert the Bruce as king of Scots. Robert's confidence was further bolstered when his second wife, Elizabeth de Burgh, gave birth to twin sons, David and John, on 5 March. Robert had a direct male heir at last. Edward II's response to this news was to give public recognition to Edward Balliol, son of King John. In November negotiations at York for a lasting peace failed, but hostilities were not resumed.

The king of Scots started building a house for his family at Cardross, near Dumbarton, overlooking the Clyde in 1325, and in the following two years of peace until 1327, he took care of political and economic matters at home and abroad. Early in 1326, one of the twin boys, John, died, and Robert's lieutenant and son-in-law, Walter Stewart, also died. At a parliament at Cambuskenneth Abbey on 15 July, the succession to the Scottish throne was again changed: Robert's remaining son David was named heir before his grandson, Robert Stewart.

In March 1325 Edward II of England's wife, Isabella and her son, the prince of Wales, had travelled to France. There she received support from her brother Charles IV to start an invasion of England to overthrow Edward II's unpopular regime, and Robert used this as an opportunity to make a formal defensive alliance with France: the Treaty of Corbeil was signed in April 1326. Queen Isabella and her lover, Sir Roger Mortimer, sailed to England unopposed in September and made for London, supported by the earls of Norfolk and Leicester.

Edward II and Hugh Despenser tried to flee to Ireland, but were captured at Glamorgan in November. The king's favourite was executed, and Edward II was imprisoned in Kenilworth Castle, where he was forced to abdicate and his son was crowned Edward III on 1 February 1327. Edward II was moved to Berkeley Castle in Gloucestershire. The deposed king was starved and ill treated. On 21 September 1327 he was declared dead, and his outwardly unmarked body was displayed for public scrutiny. The exact cause of his death is unknown but later accounts alleged that it was caused by the insertion of a red-hot poker into his rectum.

Before Edward's death in such humiliating circumstances, Robert's nephew Donald, earl of Mar, who had been a friend of Edward II, asked the Scottish king to help him free the imprisoned English king.

As part of a wider campaign to undermine Isabella and Mortimer's vulnerable regency, Robert sailed to Ulster at Easter 1327 where he claimed the earldom of his deceased father-in-law, Richard de Burgh. Robert's arrival exploited Anglo-Irish tensions and forced the English in Ireland to sign a one-year truce. At the same time, Randolph, Douglas and Mar led a Scottish army into northern England; in early September, Robert and further reinforcements joined them. The Scots surrounded Norham and Alnwick, and Robert proclaimed that he intended to annex the northern counties. Edward III and his regents could not fund another war, and they did not wish to lose part of the country, so two English envoys were sent to Norham to negotiate a lasting peace.

In October 1327, Robert proposed his terms for peace, which were quickly accepted and ratified the following year at Edinburgh and Northampton. Robert I was to be recognised as the legitimate king of Scots. He and his heirs were to have the kingdom of Scotland free of any homage, while Edward III was to renounce his claim of lordship. In return Robert I would pay Edward III £20,000 within three years. Robert's son David was to marry Edward III's sister Joan, and the marriage took place at Berwick in July 1328, although neither Robert nor Edward III attended. No one in Scotland would be allowed to hold lands in England, and vice versa. The two countries would have a military alliance, which was not to affect the Scottish alliance with France, and Edward III would use his influence to have the papal sentence of excommunication lifted.

These proposals were very similar to those that had been negotiated by Robert and Andrew Harclay in 1323.

On 17 March 1328, in a room in the guest accommodation at Holyrood Abbey in Edinburgh, where Robert lay ill, the final treaty documents were sealed and ratified. Edward III and many of his nobles thought the terms of the treaty were shameful and he tried to modify the terms. Although his mother's rule was criticised, however, he was forced to accept the treaty; as a petty act of spite, he refused to allow the Stone of Scone to be returned to Scotland.

When he seized power in 1330, Edward III then had his mother imprisoned and Mortimer executed.

After signing the treaty, Robert retired to his family house at Cardross. He had managed to travel to Ulster in August 1328, but at great cost to his health, and remained at Cardross until February 1329, growing steadily weaker. It has been suggested that Robert may have suffered from leprosy, but he maintained regular contact with friends and family until his death which would indicate his illness was not contagious.

In October 1328, the pope had finally lifted the sentence of excommunication but as Robert was a deeply pious man he sought further absolution for his crimes. In February 1329 he left Cardross and made a very slow and laboured pilgrimage to St Ninian's Shrine at Whithorn, in southern Galloway. He spent several days there, fasting and praying. When he returned to Cardross in late April, he summoned his leading Scottish nobles and asked them to swear oaths of loyalty to his son. As he had been unable to go on crusade, Robert also requested that one of them take his heart to the Holy Land; Sir James Douglas was chosen.

Robert the Bruce, king of Scots, and now widely known as Robert the

Dunfermline Abbey (see next page)

Bruce, died on 7 June 1329. His heart was given to Sir James Douglas, and his body carried in a great procession to Dunfermline Abbey, where he was buried in the choir of the abbey, near his wife, Elizabeth, who had died two years earlier on 26 October 1327.

Early in 1330, Douglas left from Berwick accompanied by six knights; from Flanders he sailed to Spain, landing at Seville. Douglas carried Robert's heart in a silver casket and was welcomed by Alfonso XI, king of Castile and Leon. When the Moors of Granada attacked Seville, Douglas's host asked him to lead the vanguard against the invaders. Unfortunately Douglas and others of his small party were killed during the battle.

Robert the Bruce's heart, and Douglas's body, were later brought back to Scotland and buried: Bruce's heart at Melrose Abbey, and Douglas's remains at St Bride's Kirk at Douglas.

Melrose Abbey

10. WHAT HAPPENED AFTER: THE LEGACY OF BANNOCKBURN

T HE BATTLE OF BANNOCKBURN was a hugely important victory for Robert and the Scots, indeed Scotland's greatest military victory, and a catastrophic defeat for the English. It broke the power of the Scottish nobles who opposed Robert I and united the kingdom behind him, but it did not bring full peace with England or force Edward II to recognise his kingship.

Even after peace was negotiated during Edward III's reign, the relationship between the Scots and English was tense. Although Robert was a strong and charismatic leader, who had secured the sovereignty of both the Scottish kingdom and its monarchy, he could not guarantee it after his death. Robert did, however, force the political community to sacrifice lands and titles in order to develop a strong united front, and a nascent concept of nationality and nationhood. He took risks, and put his own person at the centre of any decisions and actions. As a military leader he personally led attacks and maintained a clear, strong authority; as king. This meant he was hated as much as supported.

After Robert's death, the early years of David II's reign were relatively peaceful. The experienced Randolph ensured the payment of money for the treaty of Edinburgh-Northampton. Pope John XXII had authorised the use of a full coronation ceremony in 1329, and David II was anointed with holy oil at Scone in November 1331.

Robert Stewart's dealings, however, with Randolph and his nephew, the young king, were strained. There was also the legacy of the Disinherited, who waited in exile, ready to exploit any divisions or weaknesses amongst the Scots. Robert I had resisted the repeated invasions of one of the most war-like nations in Europe, but the deaths of the king, and many of his closest supporters within a couple of years, particularly Bishop Lamberton, Sir James Douglas and then Randolph, revealed the fragility of his settlement.

Civil war returned to Scotland in the early 1330s. The Mowbrays,

Statue of Robert the Bruce, King Robert I, Stirling Castle

Umfravilles, Comyns, and others, including Edward Balliol, all resented their treatment by Robert and the loss of their lands. In 1332, Balliol and others assembled a small army and made preparations to invade. As Randolph set out to face Balliol and his forces, he unfortunately died, perhaps being poisoned. Sir James Douglas, who had been Randolph's named successor, had died in Spain and the unity and strength of the Scots was undermined in the absence of strong leadership. Balliol and the Disinherited defeated a Scots army at Dupplin Moor, near Perth, on 11 August 1332. Donald, earl of Mar, led the Scots but his authority was compromised because he had previously supported Balliol. The battle was chaotic, and Mar and his main rival, Robert Bruce of Liddesdale, were both slain.

Although the Scots were shocked and dismayed at the loss of both the battle and their main leaders, over the next year they managed to resist the advances of Edward Balliol and his supporters. Unfortunately in 1333, Edward III of England then decided to provide support and sent men, ships, supplies and weapons to the north-east of England, where Balliol had taken Berwick.

The ensuing battle for the town took place at Halidon Hill. Archibald Douglas, who had been named Scottish guardian, led the Scots to a disastrous defeat and the start of nearly another decade of civil war. Edward Balliol held a parliament at Scone in September 1333 and restored the Disinherited, while David II, son of Robert the Bruce, was sent to France for his safety the following year. Despite his initial success, Balliol's reign was fragile and weak. He was unable to maintain peace and loyalty within his own main support, and David II's party, led by William Douglas, Robert Stewart and Andrew Murray, and a number of other local leaders, increasingly harassed and restricted Balliol's administration, which needed further help from Edward III.

Balliol's hold over parts of Scotland remained limited and the cost of supporting and maintaining garrisons in Scotland proved increasingly expensive for Edward III. After 1338 the English king's attention and ambitions turned to war with France. The Scottish leaders continued to fight in the name of David II, who returned to his kingdom in 1341. Although he was recognised officially as king, David faced a challenge when he tried to develop his own personal rule. Like his father, David used patronage to reward loyalty and support, but during his absence the guardians and leaders of his cause had strengthened their own positions, and some resented his return, particularly his heir, Robert Stewart, whom – it seems – David detested back.

David II led small raids into England during 1345 and 1346, but that year Edward III defeated the French at the Battle of Crécy, and Philip VI of France appealed to David and the Scots for support. David decided to escalate his campaigns to a full invasion and called a host to gather at Perth. Although the numbers that mustered indicated a good level of support for David, his leadership of the campaign was far less successful. Key commanders were in disagreement and the route taken by the Scots was inefficient and allowed the English to prepare their defences. The two sides met at Neville's Cross, near Durham, on 17 October 1346; the battle was hard and the tactics used by David and his commanders poor. The rearguard, led by Stewart and Patrick, earl of Dunbar, retreated leaving the rest of the army to be defeated and the king was taken hostage.

Some have suggested that Robert Stewart's decision to retreat at Neville's Cross was a selfish one. With the king in captivity, he was able to resume his leadership and advance his personal interests. During the years of Stewart's regime, the nobles indulged their ambitions, while at the same time ostensibly continuing the fight for the return of their king. Edward III was happy to offer David his freedom in return for David's homage; however David refused this offer to become Edward's vassal. In 1351 Edward rephrased his offer: David would be released after payment of £40,000. He would have to guarantee the restoration of the Disinherited and, in return, Edward would relinquish his Scottish lands. David was also to nominate John of Gaunt, son of the English king, as his heir instead of Robert Stewart, if David had no children of his own.

This was a compromise on which Edward III and David II agreed, but which the Scottish political community rejected in 1352. They resented the possibility that, if David died childless, the English royal family would inherit the kingdom of Scots. David's influence in Scotland was weak and Stewart was able to extend his control. During the early 1350s, centralised control over Scottish financial and political affairs was minimal.

The Scots were still involved in the wars between England and France, and the king of France, John II, encouraged them to attack and 'make war against the English'. Although the Scots took Berwick in 1355, there was tension between the joint Scottish and French leadership, and general resentment about French participation in Scottish affairs.

In response to the attack on Berwick, Edward III marched north to Lothian in January 1356 and ravaged the land around Edinburgh and Haddington during the period known as Burnt Candlemas. Ultimately his campaign in Scotland failed but, when the French king was captured near Poitiers in September 1356, efforts to reach a settlement between the Scots and English were intensified.

Terms were reached at Berwick in 1357: a ransom of £66,666 was to be paid. There was to be a ten-year truce and further negotiations for full peace; the Disinherited would not have their lands restored and the English would not be involved in the Scottish succession.

Thus it was, almost 44 years after Bannockburn, that the 1357 Treaty of Berwick marked a final end to decades of war and hostility over the sovereignty of the kingdom of Scots.

THE BATTLE OF BANNOCKBURN did not end the wars, nor did it lead to a permanent peace or even an immediate truce. Very few battles in the medieval age, of course, were ever totally decisive. Most were part of longer periods of conflict, where all sides met successes and failures, victories and defeats. Neither Stirling Bridge nor Falkirk had brought an end to the war between the Scots and English, similarly Crécy and Poitiers did not stop the fighting between the French and English.

Bannockburn did, however, mark a key point in the wars. After his victory, Robert I took the war to Edward II of England, and pursued his campaigns on English soil and beyond, rather than in Scotland. Robert's confidence was at its zenith, illustrated by his decision to fight in Ireland as well as in northern England. The victory at Bannockburn also highlighted the limits of Robert's military capabilities. In the following years Robert wisely continued to use guerrilla tactics: hit-and-run raids and scorched earth tactics rather than risk further large field battles.

In terms of economy and government, the years after Bannockburn when Robert was able to avoid the expense of pitched battles, the country was able to recover from some of the damage that had resulted from nearly 20 years of conflict. The raids into England provided money and supplies; the absence of raids by the English also meant the Scots could harvest their crops without fear of destruction. Towns were able to trade and therefore pay taxes and customs. After years of poverty and hardship, Scotland's income and people experienced a period of relative prosperity.

Bannockburn also led to the return of members of Robert's family who had been held in captivity, particularly his wife Elizabeth. The security of his succession, and the foundation of a Bruce dynasty, was something that became increasingly important after Bannockburn.

In between leading raids in England and Ireland, Robert and Elizabeth managed to spend enough time together for Elizabeth to fall pregnant, although it still took nine years. Robert was 49 when his sons were born in 1324; although suffering from ill health this must have been an occasion of great joy and relief for the king.

Robert and his supporters were able to use Bannockburn to justify his legitimate position as king of Scots: 'Robert de Brus was commonly called King of Scotland'. He had been tested in battle and the victory proved God was on his side – and on that of Scotland. The Scottish church had supported Robert since 1306, and after his success at the battle, he was keen to show his gratitude both to God and to the church. Robert promised an annual grant to the shrine of St Andrew and attended the dedication of the new cathedral at St Andrews in 1318. The victory meant the claims about Robert's godly approval issued in the name of the Scottish clergy in 1309-10 were fully justified. Bannockburn did not, however, lead to any immediate formal recognition by the pope.

The battle changed the relationship between Robert and the political community, as well as the nature of the Scottish nobility. Loyalty to Robert and his cause from the Scots had been a hard-fought struggle, and, although they did not disappear completely, threats to Robert's authority from within Scotland diminished after Bannockburn. He was able to reward and promote his followers as his position as a legitimate king became more assured. In return, those who held land from Robert, eventually had to put their loyalty to the king of Scots above personal interests and sacrifice their English estates and titles. After the parliament at Cambuskenneth in 1314, those who could not, or would not, lost their lands and properties in Scotland.

Bannockburn also changed the shape of landowning in England. Dual loyalty was a thing of the past: nobles were either loyal to Robert I of Scots or to Edward II of England, and then to Edward III. There was a clearer political boundary established between Scottish and English nobility after Bannockburn.

Bannockburn allowed Robert to capitalise on poor leadership in England and Edward II's lack of support from his nobles. The English king was increasingly unable to exert his authority and this would ultimately culminate in his murder and the 1327 peace negotiated during Isabella and Mortimer's regency.

As with other particular events or documents, some later interpretations have emphasised or mythologised the importance of Bannockburn. Certainly when placed alongside the relatively few large field battles won by the Scots compared with those they lost, Bannockburn deserves its place in the history of the country. As part of the long years of conflict known as the Wars of Independence, it also stands out as a significant event but, largely, the significance of the battle was what it enabled Robert to do after the victory.

In the final analysis, the sovereignty of the kingdom of Scotland, and the creation of a national political identity, was greatly strengthened by the Battle of Bannockburn; the battle itself was part of a much larger story.

Statue of Robert the Bruce, Bannockburn

PLACES TO VISIT

BANNOCKBURN BATTLEFIELD

Off M80/M9 at Junction 9 off A872, 2 miles S of Stirling, Bannockburn, Stirling.

The site of the momentous battle of Bannockburn, when Robert the Bruce – King Robert I – and the Scots routed the larger forces of Edward II of England on 23-24 June 1314. Features include a major new visitor centre opening in 2014, the Borestone from which Bruce is said to have had his command post, the refreshed Rotunda, and the famous equestrian statue of Robert the Bruce, which has also been restored.

NTS: Battlefield open all year, daily; new visitor centre will open in March 2014; advisable to book on line in advance. Parking. Visitor centre. Shop. Cafe. WC. Disabled access. Admission charged.
t: 0844 493 2139 p: FK7 0LJ
w: battleofbannockburn.com

ARBROATH ABBEY

Off A92, in the town of Arbroath, Angus.

The picturesque ruins of the abbey where in 1320 the influential and iconic Declaration of Arbroath was written, probably by Bernard de Linton, Bishop of Arbroath and Chancellor of Scotland. Some of the imposing abbey church remains, including the fine west end, the gatehouse, the sacristy and the Abbot's House, which has a museum.

HS: Open all year, daily. Parking. Visitor centre. Shop. Refreshments. WC. Disabled access. Herb garden. Admission charged.
t: 01241 878756 p: DD11 1EG
w: www.historic-scotland.gov.uk

BOTHWELL CASTLE

Off B7071 at Uddingston, 3 miles NW of Hamilton, Lanarkshire.

One of the largest early castles in Scotland, Bothwell saw much action in the Wars of Independence. Standing in a pretty spot above the Clyde, there are the remains of a round donjon with ditch and an impressive courtyard and towers.

HS: Open all year: Apt-Sep, daily; Oct-Mar, Sat-Wed. Parking. Shop. Refreshments. WC. Reasonable disabled access. Admission charged.
t: 01698 816894 p: G71 8BL
w: www.historic-scotland.gov.uk

CAERLAVEROCK CASTLE

Off B725, 7 miles SE of Dumfries, Caerlaverock, Dumfries and Galloway.

The castle was captured by Edward I of England in 1300 after a siege, the events commemorated in the medieval poem *'Le Siege de Karlavreock'*, but was eventually retaken by the Scots. This is a fantastic unique triangular-shaped castle with a wet moat enclosing an impressive complex of buildings.

HS: Open all year, daily. Parking. Nature trail. Shop. Cafe. WC. Limited disabled access. Admission charged.
t: 01387 770244 p: DG1 4RU
w: www.historic-scotland.gov.uk

DIRLETON CASTLE

Off A198, 2 miles W of North Berwick, Dirleton, East Lothian.

The castle was captured by the English after a hard siege in 1298. The castle is

Direlton Castle

particularly scenic and is a fascinating building to explore with a warren of chambers. There are fine grounds with colourful gardens.

HS. Open all year, daily. Parking nearby. Shop. Refreshments. WC nearby. Limited disabled access. Admission charged.

t: 01620 850330   p: EH39 5ER

w: www.historic-scotland.gov.uk

DUNFERMLINE ABBEY & PALACE

Off A994, Monastery Street, in Dunfermline, Fife.

When Edward I stayed at Dunfermline in 1303-4, he described the place as 'not a church but a den of thieves' and had it sacked and torched. Robert the Bruce's body – although not his heart – is buried in the church, on the site of the choir of the abbey, his tomb marked by a brass plaque while a plaster cast of his skull is also on display. The fine nave of the

abbey church and the ruins of the abbey buildings and palace can also be visited. Pittencrieff Park is nearby.

Dunfermline Abbey Church (site of choir), open Apr-late Oct, daily. Parking nearby. Shop. Disabled access.

t: 01383 723005   p: KY12 7PE

w: www.dunfermlineabbey.co.uk

Nave of church, abbey and palace (HS): open Apr-Sep, daily; Oct-Mar, Sat-Wed; closed for lunch. Parking nearby. Shop. Disabled access to nave but limited elsewhere. Admission charged.

t: 01383 739026   p: KY12 7PD

w: www.historic-scotland.gov.uk

DUNSTAFFNAGE CASTLE

Off A85 at Dunbeg, 3.5 miles NE of Oban, Dunstaffnage, Argyll.

The castle is on an ancient site and was a property of the MacDougalls of Lorn before they were routed and the castle captured by Robert the Bruce in 1308. In an attractive wooded spot, the imposing edifice has a mighty curtain wall with towers, which encloses buildings including the later gatehouse block. Interesting ruin of a chapel, also the burial place of the Campbells.

HS: Open Apr-Sep, daily; Oct-Mar, Sat-Wed. Parking. Gift shop. Refreshments. WC. Disabled access to grounds and shop but not into castle. Admission charged.

t: 01631 562465 p: PA37 1PZ

w: www.historic-scotland.gov.uk

EDINBURGH CASTLE

Off A1, in the centre of Edinburgh, at the top of the Royal Mile (Castlehill).

Standing on a high rock dominating the city, Edinburgh Castle was one of the strongest and most important fortresses in Scotland. The castle had an English garrison from 1296 until 1313 during the Wars of Independence, when the Scots, led by Thomas Randolph, climbed the rock, surprised the garrison, and retook it. The castle was slighted, but there was an English garrison here again until 1341. This is one of the foremost visitor attractions in Britain and the oldest building is a small Norman chapel of the early 12th century, dedicated to St Margaret, wife of Malcolm Canmore. The castle was besieged and rebuilt many times during its long and turbulent history and was developed into a daunting fortress. Among its many attractions are the views from the walls, the Scottish crown jewels, the Stone of Destiny (or Scone) on which the kings of Scots were inaugurated at Scone, the Scottish War Memorial, and the Regimental Museum of the Royal Scots. The tattoo is held on the esplanade of the castle every summer.

HS: Open all year, daily (including 1/2 Jan). Limited parking (no parking during tattoo). Shops. Restaurant and cafe. WC. Partial disabled access and mobility vehicle available. Admission charged.

t: 0131 225 9846 p: EH1 2NG

w: www.edinburghcastle.gov.uk

GLASGOW CATHEDRAL

Off M8, Castle Street (eastern end of Cathedral Street), centre of Glasgow.

This was the seat of the influential Robert Wishart, bishop of Glasgow, who was a friend of both William Wallace and Robert the Bruce. Wishart was buried in the cathedral and his stone effigy is in the crypt. Dedicated to St Mungo, Glasgow's patron saint, the present magnificent cruciform church, with a central tower and dating from the 13th century, is the only medieval cathedral on mainland Scotland to survive the Reformation more or less intact. The building is still used as the parish church of Glasgow.

HS. Open all year, daily (closed to visitors on Sun mornings and during services). Parking nearby. Shop. Limited disabled access.

t: 0141 552 6891 / 0141 552 0988

 p: G4 0QZ

w: www.historic-scotland.gov.uk / www.glasgowcathedral.org.uk

KILDRUMMY CASTLE

Off A97, 10 miles SW of Alford, Aberdeenshire.

Kildrummy was captured by Edward I of England in 1296, and then again in 1306 from a garrison led by Neil Bruce, younger brother of Robert the Bruce, after the castle was set alight by a traitor. Nigel Bruce, and the rest of the garrison, were executed by hanging. The traitor was rewarded with much gold – poured molten down his throat. In a scenic spot among the rolling hills of Aberdeenshire, this was one of the greatest stone castles in Scotland and, although very ruinous, is still an impressive edifice.

HS. Open Apr-Sep, daily. 0.5 miles walk to castle. Parking. Shop. Refreshments. WC. Limited disabled access. Admission charged.

t: 01975 571331 p: AB33 8RA

w: www.historic-scotland.gov.uk

LINLITHGOW PALACE

Off A803, in Linlithgow, West Lothian.

There was a 12th-century castle here, which was captured and strengthened by Edward I of England in 1301. It was slighted after being retaken by the Scots by driving a cart into the entrance, and remained a ruin until about 1350. The castle was repaired by David II, then rebuilt as a palace by James I. It became a favourite residence of the monarchs of Scots, and Mary, Queen of Scots, was born here. Now a spectacular ruin in a pretty spot in a park by the loch, the ruinous palace has ranges of buildings set around a rectangular courtyard. There is a fine carved working fountain in the courtyard.

HS. Open all year, daily. Parking. Shop. Refreshments. WC. Partial disabled access. Admission charged.

t: 01506 842896 p: EH49 7AL

w: www.historic-scotland.gov.uk

Linlithgow Palace

PLACES TO VISIT

MELROSE ABBEY

Off A7 or A68, in Melrose, Borders.

The abbey was attacked by the English in 1300, 1307 and 1322 (and later). Robert the Bruce's heart, which had been taken on pilgrimage by Sir James Douglas, was buried in the chapter house at Melrose. The spot is marked by a plaque. The ruins of the elegant church of Melrose Abbey are magnificent, while the rest of the buildings are very ruinous apart from the museum housed in the altered abbot's house.

Sir James Douglas, himself, died on crusade in Spain and was buried at St Bride's Church at Douglas in Lanarkshire, near his ancestral home, and his carved tomb, along with others of his family, can also be visited (contact key keeper on 01555 851657).

Melrose Abbey: HS. Open all year, daily. Parking. Shop. Picnic area. WC. Reasonable disabled access. Admission charged.

t: 01896 822562   p: TD6 9LG
w: www.historic-scotland.gov.uk

NATIONAL WALLACE MONUMENT

Off B998, 1 mile NE of Stirling Castle, Abbey Craig, Stirlingshire.

The 200-foot tower, with 246 steps, was built in 1869 to commemorate William Wallace, victor at the nearby Battle of Stirling Bridge in 1297. There are fine views towards the Highlands, and from the Forth Bridges to Ben Lomond. Wallace's two-handed sword is preserved inside, and there are displays on Wallace and other great Scots such as Robert the

Bruce, Robert Burns and Sir Walter Scott in the Hall of Heroes.

Open all year, daily (including 2 Jan), although closed some days in Jan for maintenance. Parking. Shop. Cafe. WC. Restricted disabled access because of stairs. Admission charged.

t: 01786 472140   p: FK9 5LF
w: nationalwallacemonument.com

SCONE PALACE

Off A93, 2 miles N of Perth, Scone, Perthshire.

Scone was for many centuries where the kings of Scots were inaugurated, including Robert the Bruce in 1306. The Stone of Destiny, also called the Stone of Scone, was kept here, until taken to Westminster Abbey by Edward I of England in 1296 – although the stone was returned to Edinburgh Castle in

1996. An abbey had been established at Scone from the 12th century or earlier but this was dissolved at the Reformation and replaced by an impressive castellated mansion of the Murray Earls of Mansfield. Open Apr-Oct, daily. Parking. Gift and food shops. Restaurant. Tearoom. WC. Picnic area. 100 acres of wild gardens. Maze. Adventure playground. Disabled access to state rooms & restaurant. Admission charged.

t: 01738 552300   p: PH2 6BD
w: www.scone-palace.co.uk

ST ANDREWS

Off A91, St Andrews, Fife.

This was the seat of Bishop William Lamberton, who inaugurated Robert the Bruce as king in 1306 and was a loyal and influential supporter of Bruce and Wallace before him. Lamberton was buried in the cathedral by the high altar. The cathedral was the largest and most magnificent church in Scotland, and Robert the Bruce attended the dedication of the cathedral in 1318. St Andrews was the centre for the Scottish church until the Reformation in the 1560s, after which the cathedral became very ruinous. This is still a monumental edifice, along with St Rule's Tower, the magnificent museum of early carved stones, the strong precinct wall, and the interesting graveyard. Nearby are the remains of the castle, the residence of the bishops, which saw action in the Wars of Independence but was slighted by Robert the Bruce in 1310. It was rebuilt and had a long and eventful history, not least the siege of 1546 after the murder

of Cardinal David Beaton which left a siege mine and the counter mine dug by the garrison, both of which may be entered. The town of St Andrews has many other points of interest.

HS. Cathedral and castle open all year, daily. Parking nearby. Shop. WC at castle. Reasonable disabled access. Admission charged (joint ticket available).

t: 01334 472563 (cathedral) / 01334 477196 (castle)   p: KY16 9QL
w: www.historic-scotland.gov.uk

STIRLING CASTLE

Off A872, Upper Castle Hill, in Stirling.

Edward I of England captured the castle in 1304 when he used – although after the garrison had surrendered – a siege engine called the Warwolf. William Wallace took the castle for the Scots, but it was retaken by the English until the

PLACES TO VISIT

Battle of Bannockburn in 1314. Robert the Bruce had the castle slighted, but it was rebuilt by Edward III of England, after his victory of Halidon Hill in 1333. This was one of the most important and powerful castles in Scotland, and the fortress stands on a high rock over Stirling. Features of interest include the King's Old Buildings, the Great Hall, the Chapel Royal, the kitchens, the wall walk and the nearby King's Knot, the earthworks of a magnificent garden.

HS. Open all year, daily (including 1/2 Jan). Parking. Shops. Cafe. WC. Reasonable disabled access. Admission charged.

t: 01786 450000 p: FK8 1EJ

w: www.stirlingcastle.gov.uk

STIRLING OLD BRIDGE

Off A9, N of Stirling Castle, by Customs Roundabout, off Drip Road, Stirling.
Although this bridge was built in the early 15th century, it stands on or very near the site of William Wallace's crushing victory of Stirling Bridge in 1297.
Access at all reasonable times.

URQUHART CASTLE

Off A82, 17 miles south-west of Inverness, 1.5 miles E of Drumnadrochit, Highland.
Urquhart was taken in 1296 by the English, retaken by the Scots, only to be recaptured by the English in 1303. In 1308 it was besieged and taken by the Scots, led by Robert the Bruce. The castle held out for David II in 1333. Standing in a picturesque location on Loch Ness, Urquhart Castle is now very ruinous with a curtain wall, gatehouse, hall, chapel, and tower house.

HS. Open all year, daily (including New Year). Parking. Visitor centre Shop. Cafe. WC. Limited disabled access. Admission charged.

t: 01456 450551 p: IV63 6XJ

w: www.historic-scotland.gov.uk

Please note that all sites are closed at Christmas (25/26 Dec) and at New Year (1/2 Jan) unless otherwise stated. If travelling any distance check opening with sites before setting out. The sites are all marked on the map on page 39.

Urquhart Castle